EVERYDAY GREEK

EVERYDAY GREEK

GREEK WORDS IN ENGLISH, INCLUDING SCIENTIFIC TERMS

By

HORACE ADDISON HOFFMAN

Professor Emeritus of Greek
Indiana University

THE UNIVERSITY OF CHICAGO PRESS
CHICAGO, ILLINOIS

THE UNIVERSITY OF CHICAGO PRESS, CHICAGO 60637
THE UNIVERSITY OF CHICAGO PRESS, LTD., LONDON

Copyright 1919 by The University of Chicago
All rights reserved. Published 1919. Midway Reprint 1977
Printed in the United States of America

International Standard Book Number: 0-226-34787-7

PREFACE

This book has grown out of my own needs in giving a brief course in the derivation of English words of Greek origin. I have the hope that it will also be of service to many other teachers in giving similar courses in colleges and high schools. I believe also that many persons will find such a manual very helpful for private study and reference. Those who have studied Greek in the usual way will find the book helpful for purposes of review and in the application of their knowledge to the study of Greek words in English. Others can use the book in private study as the means of acquiring in the shortest and most direct way a sufficient knowledge of Greek to enable them to trace the origin and feel the force of scientific terms and other English words of Greek origin.

The book is not intended to take the place of the English dictionary or the Greek lexicon, but only to prepare the student to make a more intelligent use of the dictionary.

One of the chief problems in preparing this manual has been to decide just what to include in it and what to leave out, so that it might contain neither too much nor too little. I have tried to strike a happy medium and to include only those things which are fundamental for the purposes of the book, selecting my examples in such a way as to illustrate the different types of words. I cannot expect to satisfy everyone by my selections. No doubt many teachers and students will find some things included which they consider superfluous, and others will miss things which they would prefer to have included. This will be especially true of the vocabulary and the lists of words given for study. It will, however, be easy for anyone to omit words and sections which he does not care to study, and those who wish different examples from those given can collect lists of words in which they, or their students, are particularly interested. It is to be hoped, indeed, that students who use this book will not confine themselves to the words given in it, but that each one, after mastering the fundamental principles and enough of the examples to illustrate them, will seek to apply his knowledge to the words of Greek derivation which belong to his own special field of study.

It will be noticed that, in so far as scientific terms are concerned, I have given a preponderance of medical terms. There are three reasons for this. In the first place, I have tried to make this work especially helpful to medical students; secondly, the medical terminology has to a considerable extent been handed down to us from the ancient Greek physicians and preserves more fully the true Greek forms and meanings than that of most other sciences; thirdly, many of these medical terms have come into general use and belong to everyday language, not merely to the professional language of the physician. Even new terms in medicine often very soon become widely known and a part of the common language of educated people. I believe, therefore, that the amount of attention given to medical terms is justified, even if the user of the book does not intend to study medicine.

I have tried to present the material in the most convenient and practical form rather than in a scientific and exhaustive form. The Greek scholar will think that I have not dug very deep in my chapter on the formation of words, or in giving the derivation of individual words. I feel, however, that I have given quite as much as the ordinary student of this book will be able to assimilate in the time which he can give to the subject.

Classes using the book should study the first three divisions —The Alphabet, Parts of Speech, and Word Formation— in the order given in the text. The matter in these divisions is arranged by topics and in what has seemed to me the best order for study. I have not divided it into lessons of definite length, and the teacher can, therefore, adapt the length of the assignments to the nature of his class and the conditions under which the work is given. The remainder of the book consists of a collection of material to be used in the application of the principles learned in the first three divisions. The order in which this is taken is of no special importance. The teacher can select from this material such portions as best suit the needs of his class and the time at their disposal. He may substitute other words and groups if he prefers.

It is a good exercise to have students collect words of Greek origin from the studies in which they are most interested, such as philosophy, botany, zoölogy, politics, etc. This will add to their interest in the work, and the words so collected may be made a basis of study in the class. Suitable passages of English may be read in class and the words of Greek origin picked out and analyzed. Such practical exercises can be extended indefinitely and will be limited only by the time at the disposal of the class. After a student has covered the first three divisions of the book the application of the principles to the analysis of words and groups of related words will be the best means of fixing those principles in mind and of making them useful to the student. Such exercises will afford a constant review of the fundamental principles and vocabulary.

The English index and key at the end of the book can be used to find all the information given in the book about any word.

HORACE A. HOFFMAN

BLOOMINGTON, INDIANA
February 17, 1919

CONTENTS

I. THE ALPHABET 1

Historical Sketch; The Greek Alphabet of the Present Time; English Pronunciation of Words of Greek Origin

II. PARTS OF SPEECH 13

Nouns; Verbs; Adjectives; Pronouns; Prepositions; Adverbs; Conjunctions

III. FORMATION OF WORDS 23

Definitions of Terms; Euphony; Vowel Changes; Some Common Suffixes; Verbal Adjectives; Denominative Adjectives; Denominative Verbs; Compound Words

IV. WORD GROUPS FOR STUDY 42

V. VOCABULARY 63

VI. INDEX AND KEY TO DERIVATION 95

I. THE ALPHABET

(The Alpha-Beta: The A-B-C's)

Historical Sketch

1. The Greek alphabet is the parent of all modern European alphabets, including our own.

The ancient Greek alphabet was derived from the Phenician alphabet. Modifications were made to some extent in the forms of the letters, and still more in the sounds for which they stood. The Phenician alphabet had no characters to represent vowel sounds, and so some of the Phenician characters which represented sounds not found in the Greek language were used by the Greeks to represent vowel sounds.

2. Our knowledge of the ancient Greek alphabet is obtained chiefly from inscriptions on such durable materials as stone, bronze, and pottery. The oldest of the preserved inscriptions date from about 600 B.C. As we come down to later times they become more and more numerous. It is interesting to compare these inscriptions and observe how the forms of the letters, and sometimes their values, varied in different periods and in different localities. Some of these variations are especially interesting because we can find in them the origin of differences which exist today in the European alphabets. Our own alphabet comes from the Roman alphabet, which originally was the Greek alphabet as found in the Chalcidian Greek colonies in Southern Italy.

3. In ancient times the capital letters only were used in both Greek and Latin. The capitals, therefore, represent the original letters, and in studying the early history of the alphabet we must confine ourselves to the capital letters. The small letters, or lower case letters, as they are called in modern printing, grew up in cursive, or rapid, writing on parchment and papyrus. We find such cursive writing used for letters, contracts, accounts, and other non-literary purposes as early as 242 B.C. But for centuries after cursive writing had come into use for non-literary documents the capitals alone were still used in formal books and in inscriptions. Our oldest manuscripts of the New Testament are written wholly in capitals.

4. At the present time ancient Greek books are printed in modern Greek type, just as ancient Latin books are printed in modern Roman type, or, as we commonly call it, English type. The alphabet, therefore, which we learn when we first study Greek is the modern Greek alphabet, and the small letters are for practical purposes of far more importance than the capitals, since the capitals are used chiefly at the begin ning of proper names, and at the beginning of paragraphs.

5. Before we pass from the consideration of the original capital letters it will be interesting to notice a few differences between the capitals in the Greek and Roman alphabets as they are used today, and to point out their origin. We find that these differences go back to differences in the ancient Greek alphabets used in different periods of time and in different localities.

For example, the Greek Rho (P) lacks the tail found in its Roman equivalent, R, and so it is the same in form as our English P, which is represented in the Greek alphabet by the character called Pi (Π). But this Roman form of R is found in many of the older Greek inscriptions, and regularly so in the inscriptions of those Greek settlements in Italy from which the Romans got their alphabet. The same is true of practically all the differences between the later Greek and Roman alphabets. The character X, which in the standard Greek alphabet has the sound of *kh*, or German *ch*, was used in the Greek settlements in Italy as equivalent to *ks*, which is its sound in Latin and English. It is also found used in this same way in many places in Greece proper, as in Laconia, Euboea, and Boeotia. The character Ⅱ in the older Greek inscriptions has the same sound as in the Roman and English alphabet, and E is used for both long and short *e*. The Ionian Greeks, however, began very early to use this character, H, to represent the long sound of *e*, and this was later adopted at Athens, so that from about 400 B.C. this character, called eta, became the common symbol for long *e*.

6. In writing with brush or pen there was a natural tendency to round off the corners of the letters, so that many letters which were originally angular became rounded, and the Roman alphabet has more of these rounded forms than the Greek. Thus the Greek Delta (▷) became *D*. One form of Gamma is ⟨, which by rounding became *C*. One common old form of Sigma is ⧸, which by rounding became *S*, while another form, made with four strokes instead of three (⧦), was modified to Σ.

The Greek Upsilon is found in ancient Greek inscriptions in two forms, V and Y. The first form was adopted by the Romans, and, eventually becoming rounded at the bottom, gives us our U. At the time when the Romans first adopted the Greek alphabet both the Greek Upsilon and the Roman *u* (*V*) had the same sound, that of *oo* in "boot." The Latin *V* retained this sound, but by the time that the Romans began to borrow Greek words in considerable numbers the sound of the Greek Upsilon had changed to that of the French *u* and the form Y had come into general use. Therefore whenever the Romans adopted a Greek word which contained Y, since they had no letter in their own alphabet to represent its sound, they retained this character in spelling the word and thereby added a new letter to the Roman alphabet, which was used, however, only in Greek words containing it. This is the origin of our English *Y*, and we have followed the fashion of the Romans by continuing to write *y* for the Greek Upsilon in words of Greek derivation, such as "psychic," "physics," "rhythm," and the like.

From the two forms of the Greek Upsilon, V and Y, we have gotten four letters in our English alphabet, *U*, *V*, *W* (double *u*), and *Y*.

7. The Greek Lambda (Λ) and the Roman L do not at first sight seem very much alike, but when in old Greek inscriptions we find Lambda turned upside down and the right limb depressed and shortened, thus L, we at once recognize the source of L.

An interesting thing which comes out in the examination of old Greek inscriptions is the fact that the Roman alphabet and our own, though derived from the Greek alphabet, have, to some extent, retained older forms than are now found in the Greek alphabet; older even than were found in the Greek alphabet used at Athens in the time of Plato and Demosthenes, although in most cases where the two alphabets differ both forms may be traced back to very ancient times.

In the letter *Q* the Roman alphabet and our own retain the old Greek and Phenician Koppa (Ϙ) which most of the Greeks discarded very early, except as a numeral, because it was superfluous, having the same sound as *K*. In our *F* we have the old Greek Digamma, which also was discarded in very early times by the Ionian Greeks, including the Athenians. In old Greek it had the sound of our *w*, but the Romans used it as an equivalent of the eastern Phi (Φ), *ph*.

The Romans had dropped Z from their alphabet, but when they began to take Greek words over into Latin they reinstated it for use in spelling Greek words which contained Zeta. This explains how it came to be at the end of the Roman alphabet, and consequently at the end of our own. How the Y came to be the next to the last letter has already been explained above.

NOTE.—Samples of Greek inscriptions and tables showing the different forms of the letters found in different periods and in different localities may be seen conveniently in Roberts' *Introduction to Greek Epigraphy*, published by the Cambridge University Press.

The Greek Alphabet of the Present Time

8. The forms of the letters here given are those which are now used in printing both ancient and modern Greek.

Characters		Names	Equivalents	
A	α	alpha	*a*	as in *father*
B	β	beta	*b*	as in *box*
Γ	γ	gamma	*g*	as in *gun*
Δ	δ	delta	*d*	as in *dog*
E	ε	epsilon	*e*	as in *met*
Z	ζ	zeta	*z*	as in *zone*
H	η	eta	*ê*	as in *fête*
Θ	θ	theta	*th*	as in *thin*
I	ι	iota	*i*	as in *machine*
K	κ	kappa	*k*	as in *keep*
Λ	λ	lambda	*l*	as in *log*
M	μ	mu	*m*	as in *man*
N	ν	nu	*n*	as in *no*
Ξ	ξ	xi	*x*	as in *ox*
O	ο	omicron	*o*	as in *obey*
Π	π	pi	*p*	as in *pin*

Characters		Names	Equivalents
P	ρ	rho	*r* as in *run*
Σ	σ s	sigma	*s* as in *sun*
T	τ	tau	*t* as in *top*
Υ	υ	upsilon	*u* as in French *u*
Φ	φ	phi	*ph* as in *physics*
X	χ	chi	*ch* as in *machen* (German)
Ψ	ψ	psi	*ps* as in *ships*
Ω	ω	omega	*o* as in *go*

PRONUNCIATION

9. The pronunciation generally in use in American colleges is an attempt to approximate that used by the ancient Athenians in the classical period. The pronunciation now used in modern Greece differs greatly from this, is much more difficult for English-speaking students, and obscures the relation between the Greek word and the English word, or words, derived from it. In this book, therefore, the general usage of American colleges is followed.

10. **The consonants.**—The consonants are, in general, pronounced like the English equivalents given in the foregoing table of the alphabet.

The following require special explanations:

γ is always pronounced like *g* in "go," except that before κ, γ, χ, or ξ it has the sound of English *ng*, and is then represented in Latin and in English by *n*. Thus ἄγγελος, *messenger*, becomes in Latin *angelus*, and in English *angel*. Other illustrations are σφίγξ, *sphinx;* ἐγκώμιον, *encomium;* βρόγχια, *bronchia;* γ is never pronounced like *g* in gin.

θ is pronounced like *th* in thin, not like *th* in this.

σ is pronounced like *s* in sun, not like *s* in his.

χ is pronounced like German *ch* in machen.

11. The vowels and diphthongs.—The vowels are pronounced as follows:

α like *a* in *father*
ε like *e* in *met*
η like *a* in *mate*
ῑ like *e* in *me*
ῐ like *i* in *pin*
ο like *o* in *obey*
υ like French *u*, or German *ü*
ω like *o* in *go*

Theoretically the short vowels differ from the long in quantity only, that is in the length of time the sound is dwelt upon. This distinction is practically impossible for English-speaking persons, and the sounds indicated in the above table will answer our purposes.

12. Following is a table of the diphthongs and their approximate pronunciation:

αι like *i* in *mine*
ει like *ei* in *eight*
οι like *oi* in *oil*
αυ like *ou* in *out*
ευ like *eu* in *feud*
ου like *oo* in *boot*
υι like *ui* in *quit*

Besides these there are the so-called improper diphthongs, ᾳ, ῃ, ῳ, with the ι written under a long open vowel. This ι is called iota subscript, and is silent, so that these improper diphthongs are pronounced the same as ᾱ, η, ω. The iota subscript is omitted in English derivatives.

13. *Breathings.*—Every vowel or diphthong at the beginning of a word has either the rough breathing (ʽ) or the smooth breathing (ʼ). The rough breathing is pronounced

like the English *h*, the smooth breathing is not pronounced at
all and may be considered merely ornamental. The rough
breathing was also used with initial rho.

Examples: ῥόδον, *rose*.

14. *Accents.*—There are three marks of accent: the acute
('), the grave (`), and the circumflex (῀). There are compli-
cated rules for determining which accent shall be used and
where it shall be placed, but all we need to know for our purpose is that in pronouncing Greek words we accent the syllable
over which the accent is placed and make no distinction with
regard to the kind of accent mark used. The vowel which
has a circumflex over it is long.

15. Suggestions in pronunciation.—There are no silent
letters in Greek except the iota subscript. There is a syllable
for each vowel or diphthong. In trying to pronounce Greek
words, think not of the names of the Greek letters, but of the
corresponding English letters with the sounds indicated above.

16. Pronounce the words in the following list; also write
them out in Greek letters. Then transliterate these words,
that is, write them in the corresponding Roman, or English,
letters.

Learn the meanings of these words and tell what English
words you think are derived from them.

ᾠδή, *song*	ποταμός, *river*
αὐτός, *self*	ἄνθρωπος, *human being, man*
φόβος, *fear*	ὁδός, *road, way*
νέκταρ, *nectar*	μέτρον, *measure*
φωνή, *sound, voice*	τόπος, *place*
νεκρός, *dead body, corpse*	πολίτης, *citizen*
ἄγγελος, *messenger*	δεσπότης, *master* (of slaves)
γράφω, *I write*	φίλος, *friend, lover*
ἵππος, *horse*	ἐπιστολή, *letter*

παράδεισος, *park*
ἀκμή, *highest point, prime*
θεός, *a god, God*
φάλαγξ, *line of battle*
ἄστρον, *star*
χείρ, *hand*
ἔργον, *work*
στρατηγός, *general*
ἀνατομή, *dissection*
βοτάνη, *grass, vegetation*
ἡμέρα, *day*
κλέπτω, *I steal*
κρατήρ, *mixing bowl*

βάσις, *step, foundation*
βίος, *life*
ὥρα, *season, hour*
ἀθλητής, *contestant*
βάρος, *weight*
δένδρον, *tree*
σφαῖρα, *ball*
ιατρός, *healer, physician*
μέγα, *large, big, great*
μικρός, *small*
εἰρήνη, *peace*
θώραξ, *breast-plate, breast, chest*
πόλις, *city, state*

Write the following words in Greek letters:
Analysis, genesis, skeleton, synthesis, parenthesis, sepsis, diagnosis, idea, pathos, embryo(n), Philadelphia, Socrates.

TRANSLITERATION

17. The first Greek words came into English through Latin and retained the Latin spelling. Thus the custom was established of spelling Greek words in English as they were spelled in Latin, not merely using the Roman characters instead of the Greek characters, but also making such changes in the letters as the Romans made in order to represent the Greek sounds by the letters and combinations of letters used to represent those sounds in Latin. Greek endings were also changed to corresponding Latin endings. Furthermore, the Latin ending is often dropped in English, or a familiar English ending substituted. Thus "dramaticus" becomes *dramatic*, "poeta," *poet*, "philosophia," *philosophy*, "nauticus," *nautical*, "practicus," *practical*. The familiar English adjective ending -*al* is itself from the Latin ending -*alis* in such words as "navalis," *naval*.

18. For the reason already explained in section 6 the Greek upsilon (Υ) was retained in Greek words taken over into Latin, and this gives us our English *Y, y*. The Greek upsilon is therefore represented by *y* when Greek words containing upsilon are written in Latin or in English, unless the upsilon is part of a diphthong, in which case it is transliterated as *u*. Thus ἀνάλυσις is written *analysis*, but ναυτικός is "nauticus" in Latin, *nautical* in English.

19. Most of the Greek consonants are transliterated by the Latin or English equivalents given in the table of alphabet (see p. 5).

κ, however, is usually transliterated as *c*.

ρ at the beginning of a word always has the rough breathing in Greek and becomes *rh* in Latin and in English. Thus ῥήτωρ becomes *rhetor*.

γ before κ, γ, χ, or ξ becomes *n*. Thus: ἄγγελος, *angelus, angel; σφίγξ, sphinx; ἐγκέφαλος, encephalus; ἐγχειρίδιον, enchiridion*.

20. The largest number of changes occur in the case of the diphthongs. These are indicated in the following table:

Greek αι becomes in Latin *ae*
Greek ει becomes in Latin *i*, occasionally *ē*
Greek οι becomes in Latin *oe*
Greek ου becomes in Latin *ū*

The older English followed the Latin spelling, but in the simplified spelling of English in recent years *ae* and *oe* have generally been shortened to *e*. Thus φαινόμενον, formerly spelled *phaenomenon*, is now generally written *phenomenon*. οἰκονομία was formerly written *oeconomy*, but is now written *economy*.

There is also a tendency in recent years in making new scientific terms to retain the Greek spelling in some cases instead of using the Latin spelling. In these instances *k* is used for κ, *ou* for ου, *ai* for αι, *ei* for ει, and *oi* for οι.

However, in tracing the derivation of most English words of Greek origin it is necessary to take into account the Latin spelling of Greek words. This is especially true of the older and better known words.

21. These peculiarities of transliteration may be summarized as follows:

κ = *c*, ῥ = *rh*, υ = *y*, αι = *ae*, ει = *ī*, or *ē*, οι = *oe*, ου = *ū*.

22. The Greek *endings* were also usually changed to the corresponding Latin endings. The most important instances for our purpose are the change of *-os* in Greek nouns and adjectives of the *o*-declension to the corresponding Latin ending *-us*, and of the neuter ending *-ov* of the same declension to the corresponding Latin ending *-um*.

Thus χόρος is *chorus* in Latin and English; Κῦρος is *Cyrus*. In English, however, the ending may be dropped altogether. Thus: μῦθος, Latin *mythus*, English *myth*.

Examples of neuters are: Μουσεῖον, *museum;* στέρνον, *sternum*; γυμνάσιον, *gymnasium*.

English Pronunciation of Words of Greek Origin

23. While Greek words are usually taken into English in a Latinized form, they are pronounced as English words with the usual English sounds of the letters. The Greek accent is disregarded both in Latin and in English, but the Latin accent is very commonly retained in English; always so in proper names. It is, therefore, important to recall the rules for the accent of Latin words, which are as follows:

Words of two syllables are always accented on the first syllable. Words of more than two syllables are accented on the next to the last syllable (penult), if that is long in quantity; otherwise on the preceding syllable (antepenult).

24. The following points should also be noted in the English pronunciation of Greek derivatives:

κ becomes *c*, which in Latin is pronounced like *k*, but in English *c* is pronounced like *s* before *e*, *i*, and *y*. Likewise *g* is pronounced like *j* before *e*, *i*, and *y*.

Examples: catalog, cycle, criticize, Cassandra, Cyrus, Cato, Cicero, genesis, galaxy, geometry, trigonometry, Ganymede, George.

Greek χ is transliterated as *ch*, but this *ch* is generally pronounced like *k*.

Examples: anarchy, chromatic, architect, technical. "Archbishop" and a few other similar words form an exception.

Greek ψ, equivalent to *ps*, is very common at the beginning of Greek words. Since we cannot easily pronounce *ps* at the beginning of a word, we drop the *p* and pronounce the *s* only.

Examples: psalm, psychology, pseudonym.

The vowels are pronounced with the usual English sounds.

EXERCISE IN TRANSLITERATION AND PRONUNCIATION

25. Write the following words both in Greek and in their Latinized English forms. Pronounce them both in Greek and in English:

Σωκράτης	Ἡρόδοτος	χόρος
Ἀριστείδης	Φοίβη	ἄγγελος
Θουκυδίδης	Κῦρος	μουσεῖον
Ἀπόλλων	ὑπόθεσις	κριτήριον
Ἀθηνᾶ	κρίσις	στέρνον
Ἀφροδίτη	γένεσις	δρᾶμα
Σοφοκλῆς	ἀκμή	κλῖμαξ
Εὐριπίδης	ᾠδή	γεωμετρία
Αἰσχύλος	χίμαιρα	φιλοσοφία
Πλάτων	Βορέας	οἰκονομία
Ἐπίκουρος	κόσμος	βακτήρια
Εὐκλείδης	μῦθος	δημοκρατία

II. PARTS OF SPEECH

26. The parts of speech in Greek are the same as in English, namely: nouns, adjectives, pronouns, verbs, adverbs, conjunctions, and prepositions. The first four are inflected, that is, they have different forms to indicate different cases, numbers, genders, persons, tenses, voices, and modes. Greek is a highly inflected language, even more so than Latin, and the number of forms is very great, especially in the verbs. These different forms are produced mainly by different endings, but to some extent by prefixes and other changes in the stem.

For our purposes it is not necessary to learn the inflections, but only such changes of forms as reappear in English words derived from the Greek. These changes are such as belong to word-formation, the process by which new stems and words are formed from existing roots and stems. The study of roots[1] and stems[1] is therefore important.

Nouns

27. The form in which we learn a Greek noun is the nominative case singular number. This is the form given first in dictionaries.

28. Declensions.—There are three declensions of Greek nouns, the *a*-declension, the *o*-declension, and the consonant declension, which are generally called the first, second, and third declensions respectively.

29. The first, or a-declension.—In this declension the stem ends in -*a*, often modified to η. The nominative singular

---

[1] For definitions of these terms see sections 55 and 56.

13

of feminine nouns of this declension ends in a or η. Masculine nouns add s.

30. The following list of words will illustrate the a-declension. These words and their meanings should be learned. Words have been selected for the list which have English derivatives, and these English derivatives will assist in remembering the Greek words and their meanings.

ὦρα, *season*, hour
ἀκμή, *highest point, prime,* acme
ᾠδή, *song,* ode
ἰδέα, *appearance, form,* idea
ἱστορία, *inquiry, information, narrative,* history
μηχανή, *contrivance, machine;* (English derivative, mechanical)
σχολή, *leisure,* (school)
φωνή, *voice, sound,* (phonetic, phonograph, telephone)
σφαῖρα, *ball,* sphere
δίαιτα, *mode of life,* (diet)

ὑγίεια, *health,* (hygiene)
κριτής, *judge,* (critic)
Βορέας, *north-wind,* (boreal)
πολίτης, *citizen,* (political)
δεσπότης, *master of slaves,* despot
ποιητής, *maker, composer,* poet
ἀθλητής, *contestant* in games, athlete
ὑποκριτής, *actor,* (hypocrite)
φιλοσοφία, *love of wisdom,* philosophy
γενέα, *race, stock, family,* (genealogy)

31. The second declension, or o-declension.—The stem ends in o. In the nom. sing. masculines and feminines add s, neuters add ν. There are very few feminines.

32.   LIST OF WORDS OF THE O-DECLENSION

ἄγγελος, *messenger,* (angel)
ἀδελφός, *brother,* (Philadelphia)
ἄνθρωπος, *man, human being,* (anthropology)
ἀριθμός, *number,* (arithmetic)
αὐλός, *pipe,* (hydraulic)

δρόμος, *road, race-track,* (hippodrome)
ἥλιος, *sun,* (heliograph, heliotrope)
θεός, *god,* (theology, theism)
ἵππος, *horse.* (hippodrome)

κόσμος, order, universe, world, (cosmopolitan)

λίθος, stone, (monolith, lithograph)

μῦθος, story, (myth)

τύπος, impress, type

νόσος (fem.), disease, (nosology)

γνάθος (fem.), jaw, (prognathous)

ὁδός, (fem.), way, journey, (exodus)

μέτρον, measure, (meter, thermometer)

σκῆπτρον, staff, scepter

δένδρον, tree, (rhododendron)

θέατρον, theater

στέρνον, breast, breast-bone, (sternum)

μουσεῖον, temple of the muses, (museum)

ὄργανον, instrument, organ

φάρμακον, drug, (pharmacy)

33. The third declension, or consonant declension.— In this declension the stem ends in a consonant, or in one of the close vowels, ι, υ. The genitive case in this declension adds -ος to the stem and the stem may generally be found by dropping this ending in the genitive. It is therefore usually necessary to know the genitive case to find the stem of those nouns whose stem ends in a consonant. Stems in ι, or υ, if masculine or feminine, add sigma in the nominative singular and the stem can be found in such words by dropping this sigma. A few stems in upsilon are neuter and have the nominative singular like the stem.

The genitive singular of nouns in this declension is given in the dictionaries and vocabularies. The nominative singular of nouns of this declension has various endings which we learn in learning the word as we find it in the dictionary or vocabulary.

34. SOME TYPICAL WORDS OF THE THIRD DECLENSION

ἀήρ, genitive ἀέρ-ος, air; (aeronaut)

δαίμων, δαίμον-ος, deity; (demon)

δέρμα, δέρματ-ος, skin; (dermatology, pachyderm)

δρᾶμα, δράματ-ος, action, deed; (drama, dramatic)

κανών, κανόν-ος, straight-edge, rule, standard; (canon)

κλῖμαξ, κλίμακ-ος, ladder, staircase; (climax)

δόγμα, δόγματ-ος, opinion, conviction, decree; (dogma)

κρατήρ, κρατῆρ-ος, mixing-bowl, bowl; (crater)

λάρυγξ, λάρυγγ-ος, larynx

πῦρ, πυρ-ός, fire; (pyrotechnic)

ῥίς, ῥιν-ός, nose; (rhinology, rhinoceros)

φῶς, φωτ-ός, light; (photograph)

χείρ, χειρ-ός, hand; (chirography)

οὖς, ὠτ-ός, ear; (otology)

γίγας, γίγαντ-ος, giant; (gigantic)

ὄρνις, ὄρνιθ-ος, bird; (ornithology)

ἧπαρ, ἥπατ-ος, liver; (hepatic)

φλέψ, φλεβ-ός, vein; (phlebotomy)

θρίξ, τριχ-ός, hair; (trichina, trichoblast; found in many scientific terms)

πούς, ποδ-ός, foot; (tripod, antipodes, polypous)

παῖς, παιδ-ός, child; (pedagogue, pediatric)

35. **Words with stems ending in ι, or υ.**—In these words the genitive is often irregular, but the nominative is regular and the stem is best found by dropping the nominative singular ending -s. The genitive of this class of words is not given in the vocabularies of this book.

36.

πόλι-s, town, city, state; (political, necropolis)

δύναμι-s, power, force; (dynamic, dynamite)

ἰχθύ-s, fish; (ichthyology)

φύσι-s, nature; (physical)

γένεσι-s, birth, origin, genesis

βάσι-s, foundation, base, basis

ναῦ-s, ship; (nausea, nautical)

ἀνάλυσι-s, analysis

σύνθεσι-s, synthesis

37. **Neuter nouns in -os.**—A special and important class of nouns in the consonant declension are the neuters with nominative in -os. All masculine and feminine nouns ending in -os belong to the o-declension, but neuter nouns in -os belong to the consonant declension. The latter originall‚ had stems ending in -es. The ε of the stem is changed tu

o in the nominative, accusative, and vocative. In the other
cases the final σ of the stem is dropped before the case
ending so that the stem seems to end in ε.

38. EXAMPLES OF NEUTER NOUNS IN -ος

γένος, γένε(σ)-ος, *race, kind;* (homogeneous, heterogeneous)
πάθος, πάθε(σ)-ος, *feeling, suffering, disease;* (pathology)
βάρος, *weight;* (barometer)
ἄνθος, *flower;* (anther, polyanthous, anthology)
εἶδος, *appearance, form, kind;* (kaleidoscope, spheroid = σφαιρο-ειδής)
ψεῦδος, *falsehood;* (pseudonym, pseudo-science)
κράτος, *power, rule;* (democratic)

Verbs

39. The form of the verb given first in dictionaries is
usually the first person singular of the present indicative
active. Thus: γράφω, *I write;* δίδωμι, *I give.* Some English
dictionaries in referring to Greek verbs give the infinitive, and
for that reason it is well to know how the infinitive ends also.

40. The most common class of verbs are those whose first
form ends in -ω, and whose present active infinitive ends in
-ειν. Thus: γράφω, *I write;* γράφειν, *to write.* In many of
these the verb stem may be found by merely dropping the
ending -ω, or -ειν. But in many other verbs the simple verb
stem has been modified in some way in the present so that it
is more or less disguised. Thus: πράσσω, *I do, I accomplish.*
Here the verb stem is not πρασσ, but πραγ, as seen in πραγματικός, English **pragmatic.** The stem is the important part
for us in tracing derivatives. Accordingly, in this book
whenever the simple verb stem cannot be found by merely
dropping the ending, the stem is placed after the verb in
parentheses. Thus: πράσσω (πραγ), *I do, accomplish.* This
stem should be learned in learning the verb since it is essential
for our purpose to know the stem.

41. Verbs in -ω with infinitive in -ειν.—

γράφω, *I write, draw, paint*
γράφειν, *to write, draw, paint;*
  (**geography, photograph**)
λύω, *I loose*
λύειν, *to loose;* (**electrolysis**)
> NOTE.—In the rest of this list the infinitive is not given and the subject "I" is omitted in the translation for the sake of brevity. The same practice will hereafter generally be observed.

δράω, *do, act;* (**drama**)
ποιέω, *make, compose;* (**poet**)
ὁράω, *see;* (**panorama**)
τρέπω, *turn;* (**tropic**)
φέρω, *bear, carry;* (**phosphorous, semaphore**)

πράσσω (πραγ), *do, accomplish,* (**pragmatic, practical**)
γι-γνώ-σκω (γνω), *know;* (**agnostic**)
κρίνω (κρι), *judge, decide;* (**crisis, critic**)
κρύπτω (κρυφ), *hide;* (**cryptogram**)
πέπτω (πεπ), *digest;* (**dyspepsia, pepsin**)
τέμνω (τεμ), *cut;* (**microtome**)
τύπτω (τυπ), *strike;* (**type**)
σχίζω (σχιδ), *split;* (**schism**)
σήπω, *rot, decay;* (**sepsis, septic**)
τείνω (τεν), *stretch;* (**tone**)

42. Verbs in -μι.

—Several important verbs end in -μι in the first person singular of the active indicative. The infinitive of these ends in -ναι.

τί-θη-μι (θε), infinitive τι-θέ-ναι, *put, place;* (**thesis, synthesis**)
δί-δω-μι (δο), infinitive δι-δό-ναι, *give;* (**dose, antidote**)
ἵ-στη-μι (στα), infinitive ἱ-στά-ναι, *stand;* (**static, system**)

43. Deponent verbs.

—In Greek there are many so-called deponent verbs which have the forms of the middle or passive voice, but are either active or intransitive in meaning. The middle and passive voices have the same form in the present tense. In the first person singular of the indicative they end in -ομαι instead of -ω. The infinitive ends in -εσθαι.

αἰσθάνομαι (αἰσθ), αἰσθάνεσθαι, *perceive;* (**aesthetic, anesthetic**)
γίγνομαι, for γι-γέν-ομαι (γεν), *become, be born;* (**genesis, eugenic**)
μιμέ-ομαι, *imitate;* (**mimetic, mimeograph**)
σκέπτομαι (σκεπ), *look at, examine, consider;* (**skeptic, telescope**)

44. Sometimes the active form has one meaning and the middle or passive another.

φαίνω (φαν), *show;* (**hierophant**).   φαίνομαι, *appear;* (**phenomenon**)

A few deponent verbs omit the vowel *o* or ε before the endings.

δύνα-μαι (δυνα), δύνα-σθαι, *be able, have power;* (**dynamic, dynasty**)

45. There are also verbal roots which are not used in the present tense, but occur in other tenses. Nouns and adjectives are often derived from such roots, and some of these roots give us common English derivatives and are important for our purposes. In these cases it will answer our purpose to learn merely the root and its meaning.

Root φαγ, *eat;* (**sarcophagus, ichthyophagous**).
Root ὀπ, *see;* (**optics, autopsy**).

Adjectives

46. Adjectives have the same declensions as nouns. They generally have different forms for different genders. Many adjectives have the feminine in the *a*-declension and the masculine and neuter in the *o*-declension.

EXAMPLES

Masculine	Feminine	Neuter
μικρός	μικρά	μικρόν, *small;* (**microscope, microtome**)
σοφός	σοφή	σοφόν, *wise;* (**sophomore, philosopher**)
μόνος	μόνη	μόνον, *alone, single;* (**monotone, monogamy**)

47. Some adjectives have the feminine in the *a*-declension and the masculine and neuter in the consonant declension. Others are declined wholly in the *o*-declension or in the consonant declension, the masculine and feminine being alike in form.

The differences in form which mark gender rarely appear in English derivatives, and for our purposes it is sufficient in most instances to learn merely the first form of the masculine and its stem. In so far as the forms of adjectives are concerned we can apply to them what we have already learned about nouns.

EXAMPLES

μικρό-s, *small;* (micro-scope, micro-cosm)
μόνο-s, *alone, single;* (mono-syllable, mono-gram)
μέγα-s, μεγάλη, *big, large;* (mega-phone, megalo-mania)
πολύ-s, *much,* plur. *many;* (poly-theism, poly-technic)
πᾶς, gen. παντ-ός, neut. πᾶν, *all;* (pan-theism, panto-mime)
μέλας, gen. μέλαν-os, *black;* (melan-choly, melan-urus)
ὁμό-s, *same;* (homo-geneous, homo-logous)
αὐτό-s, *self;* (auto-graph, auto-matic)
ἄριστο-s, *best;* (aristo-cracy)
νέο-s, *new, young;* (neo-lithic, neo-phyte)

48. The article.—The Greek has an article corresponding to the English definite article *the.* It is declined in full in each of the three genders. We need learn only the three forms of the nominative singular, as follows: masc. ὁ, fem. ἡ, neut. τό.

These forms of the Greek article are used after nouns in Greek dictionaries as a convenient way of indicating the gender of the nouns. Thus:

κριτής, ὁ, indicates that κριτής is masculine.
ὁδός, ἡ, indicates that ὁδός is feminine.
γένος, τό, indicates that γένος is neuter.

Pronouns

49. The Greek personal pronouns do not appear in English derivatives, with the exception of ἐγώ, *I,* which is found in egoism, egotism, egoistic, and egotistic.

Prepositions

50. The Greek prepositions nearly all appear in English words, some of them very frequently, and they are very important for our purposes. They are not inflected. They are very common as the first part of a compound word.

51. The following list should be learned with the meanings there given. The meanings given are chiefly those which the prepositions have in compound words, since the Greek prepositions appear in English only as parts of compound words.

ἀμφί, *about, on both sides;* (amphi-theater, amphibious)
ἀνά, *up, throughout;* (anatomy, anathema, analysis)
ἀντί, *opposite, against;* (antidote, anti-German)
ἀπό, *from, away from;* (apostasy, apology)
διά, *through;* (diameter, diaphragm)
ἐν, *in, at;* (enhydrous, energy, encaustic).
ἐκ, ἐξ, *out of;* (eccentric, exodus).
ἐπί, *upon;* (epidermis, epidemic, epitaph, epigram)
κατά, *down;* (cataract, catastrophe, cataclysm)
μετά, *after, differently;* (metacarpus, metamorphose)
παρά, *by, beside;* (parasite, paragraph)
περί, *around;* (perimeter, pericarp)
πρό, *for, before, forth;* (prologue, prophet)
σύν, *with, together;* (synthesis, sympathy)
ὑπέρ, *above, over, beyond,*(hypercritical, hyperbole, hypertrophy)
ὑπό, *under,* Latin *sub;* (hypodermic, hypothesis)

Adverbs

52. The following adverbs appear in English words:

ἔξω, *outside;* (exoteric, exogen)
ἔσω, *within;* (esoteric)
ἔνδον, *within;* (endogen)
εὖ, *well;* (euphony, eugenic)
τῆλε, *far;* (telegraph, telepathy)

53. Inseparable particles.—There are a few prefixes which are common in composition with other words, but which never occur as separate words. They are as follows:

ἀν-, ἀ- are negative like *un-* in English, or *in-* in Latin. ἀν- is used before words beginning with a vowel, ἀ- before words beginning with a consonant. Thus: an-esthetic, a-pathetic, an-odyne, a-septic.

δυσ- has the meaning *ill, bad*. It is the opposite of εὖ, *well, good*.

Examples: *dyspepsia, dysentery.*

ἡμι-, *half;* (hemisphere).

δι-, *two, double;* (diphthong, dimeter, dilemma).

καλλι-, *beautiful;* (calligraphy, calisthenics).

Conjunctions

53a. The Greek conjunctions do not appear in English derivatives and we can disregard them.

III. FORMATION OF WORDS

54. New and longer words are formed very freely in Greek from the shorter words, or rather, from their roots and stems. Most of the longer words are made up of a number of distinct parts each of which has its own special significance. Before proceeding further with the process of word-building it is necessary to learn the meaning of a few terms which we must use repeatedly.

Definitions of Terms

55. Root.—A root is the fundamental part of a word, or a group of related words. Longer stems and words may be derived from the root, but the root cannot itself be derived from any more simple element existing in the language.

Thus in **genesis, genetic, eugenic, hydrogen, endogen,** etc., there is a common syllable **gen** which is the root, meaning *become,* or *be born.* The same root with the vowel ε changed to *o* appears in other words, such as theogony, cosmogony, **gon**ophore.

The root **the,** *put,* or *place,* appears in each of the following words: **Thesis, theme,** synthesis, antithesis, apothecary, hypothetical, anathema.

56. Stem.—The stem is the part of a word which remains the same in a group of forms arising from inflection. Roots are often used as stems, but most stems consist of the root lengthened out by something added to it or prefixed to it.

Thus in **genesis,** Greek γένεσις, the root is γεν, but the stem is γενεσι. To this we add the case ending ς in the nominative and get the form γένεσις; the accusative case is γένεσιν.

57. Suffix.—A suffix is one or more syllables added to the end of a root or stem to make a new stem. The suffixes do not occur as separate words. They may be illustrated in English by the syllable -*er* in such words as sing-*er*, work-*er*, build-*er;* or by -*ness* in such words as sweet-*ness*, weari-*ness*, idle-*ness*.

58. Prefix.—A prefix is one or more syllables placed before a stem. Most of the prefixes are prepositions or adverbs, which may occur as independent words, but there are some prefixes which do not occur as separate words. (See section 53 above). We may illustrate the use of the prefix by the following English words: *un*-wise, *in*-human, *anti*-Christian.

59. Verbal.—A verbal is a word derived from a verb-stem or root. Words derived directly from roots are also called primitives.

60. Denominative.—A denominative is a word derived from the stem of a noun or an adjective.

61. Simple word.—A simple word is one formed from a single root or stem.

62. Compound word.—A compound word is formed by combining two or more stems.

Euphony

63. A great many changes are made in the spelling of Greek words for the sake of euphony (Greek εὐφωνία, *good sound*, from εὖ, *good*, and φωνή, *sound*).

To explain these euphonic changes it is necessary first to understand the classification of the Greek consonants.

CLASSIFICATION OF CONSONANTS

64. Following are the classes of consonants:

(1). Mutes, or Stops.—These may best be given in the form of a table.

25

	Surds	Sonants	Aspirates
Labials,	π	β	φ
Palatals,	κ	γ	χ
Linguals,	τ	δ	θ

In the surds the *breath* is stopped by the organs of speech, and in the sonants the *voice* is stopped in the same way. The aspirates consist of the surds followed by the aspirate sound *h*.

(2). Liquids.—λ, μ, ν, ρ. These are so called from their smooth, flowing sounds.

(3). Sibilant. σ, s.

(4). Double consonants. ζ = dz, ξ = ks, ψ = ps.

EUPHONIC CHANGES OF CONSONANTS

65. Before τ a labial or palatal mute must be co-ordinate, that is, in the same column with τ in the above table. Thus the root πραγ, *do*, with the suffix -τικος becomes not πραγ-τικός, but πρακ-τικός, **practical**. So ἐχ-τικός becomes ἐκ-τικός, **hectic**, and ἐπιληβ-τικός becomes ἐπιληπ-τικός, **epileptic**.

66. Before τ a lingual mute becomes σ. πλατ-τικός becomes πλασ-τικός, **plastic**; σχολαδ-τικός becomes σχολασ-τικός, **scholastic**.

67. Before μ a labial mute becomes μ, a palatal mute becomes γ, and a lingual mute becomes σ. γράφ-μα changes to γράμ-μα, from which we have the syllable *gram* in telegram, program, grammar, etc.; παράδεικ-μα changes to παράδειγ-μα, **paradigm**; σόφιδ-μα changes to σόφισ-μα, **sophism**; πλάτ-μα becomes πλάσ-μα, **plasm**.

68. Before a labial mute ν becomes μ. συν-πάθεια, from συν and πάθος, becomes συμ-πάθεια, **sympathy**. Compare symphysis, symphony.

69. π, β, or $\phi + \sigma = \psi$

κ, γ, or $\chi + \sigma = \xi$

τ, δ, or $\theta + \sigma = \sigma$, that is, a lingual mute is dropped before sigma.

70. ν is dropped before σ. $\sigma\acute{\upsilon}\nu$-$\sigma\tau\eta\mu\alpha$ becomes $\sigma\acute{\upsilon}$-$\sigma\tau\eta\mu\alpha$, **system.** ν is usually assimilated before μ and λ. Thus $\sigma\upsilon\nu$-$\lambda\alpha\beta\acute{\eta}$ becomes $\sigma\upsilon\lambda$-$\lambda\alpha\beta\acute{\eta}$, **syllable**; $\sigma\upsilon\nu$-$\mu\epsilon\tau\rho\acute{\iota}\alpha$, $\sigma\upsilon\mu$-$\mu\epsilon\tau\rho\acute{\iota}\alpha$, **symmetry.**

71. Initial $\acute{\rho}$ is doubled when a short vowel comes before it in the formation of a compound word. This double rho ($\rho\acute{\rho}$) comes into English as *rrh*.

Thus: $\acute{\rho}\acute{\epsilon}\omega$, *flow*, with the preposition $\kappa\alpha\tau\acute{\alpha}$ becomes $\kappa\alpha\tau\alpha\rho$-$\acute{\rho}\acute{\epsilon}\omega$, *flow down*, whence $\kappa\alpha\tau\acute{\alpha}\rho\rho\omicron\omicron s$, *a down-flowing, a running down* of mucus from the head, English **catarrh.**

71a. The only consonants which can stand at the end of a Greek word are ν, ρ, and *s*.

Vowel Changes

72. The vowel in a root or stem is often changed to some other vowel. Such changes are found also in English words not of Greek origin. Thus: Sing, sang, sung, song; sit, sat, set, seat; tell, told, tale.

In Greek the most common change of this kind is the change of ϵ in a verbal root to $\omicron$ when a noun or adjective is formed from the same root. Thus: $\tau\rho\acute{\epsilon}\pi\omega$, *turn*, $\tau\rho\omicron\pi\acute{\eta}$, *a turning, solstice*, **tropic**; $\acute{\eta}\lambda\iota\omicron$-$\tau\rho\acute{\omicron}\pi\omicron s$, *turning to the sun*, **heliotrope** ($\acute{\eta}\lambda\iota\omicron\tau\rho\acute{\omicron}\pi\iota\omicron\nu$); $\tau\epsilon\acute{\iota}\nu\omega(\tau\epsilon\nu)$, *stretch*, $\tau\acute{\omicron}\nu\omicron s$, *stretch of the string*, **tone.**

Many other vowel changes occur in Greek stems, both in the formation of tenses in the verbs and in the formation of nouns and adjectives from verb stems.

73. A final short vowel is usually lengthened before a suffix beginning with a consonant. Both ε and α become η. ποιέ-ω, ποιη-τής; ἀρθρό-ω, ἄρθρω-σις:ἵστημι(στα), σύ-στη-μα, system.

74. A final vowel is usually dropped before a suffix beginning with a vowel. μοῦσα, μουσ-ικός:νέφρο-s, νεφρ-ῖτις.

Some Common Suffixes

75. **Verbal Nouns.**—The simplest and most common suffixes by which nouns are formed from verb stems are -α and -ο, forming respectively noun stems of the α-declension and the ο-declension. The nominative case of these words ends in -α, -η, -ος, -ον. An ε in the verbal root is regularly changed to ο. The meanings vary.

πέμπω, send, escort:πομπ-ή, an escort, a procession (Eng. deriv. pomp)

τρέπω, turn:τροπ-ή, a turning, solstice, (tropic)
　　　　τρόπ-ος, turn, manner, turn, or figure of speech, trope

τέμνω (τεμ), cut:τομ-ή, a cutting, a section
　　　　τόμ-ος, section of a book, volume, tome

ἀνα-τέμνω, cut up, dissect:ἀνα-τομ-ή, dissection, anatomy

τείνω (τεν), stretch:τόν-ος, a stretching, tension, tone

76. Agent nouns are made with the suffixes -της, -τηρ, -τωρ.

ποιέω, make, compose:ποιη-τής, maker, composer, poet
ῥε, root meaning speak:ῥή-τωρ, speaker, orator, rhetor
κεράννυμι (κερα; κρα), mix:κρα-τήρ, mixer, mixing-bowl, crater
ἀθλέω, contend in games:ἀθλη-τής, contestant, athlete

77. Action nouns are made with the suffixes -σις, -σια, -μος.

κρίνω (κρι), judge, decide:κρί-σις, decision, crisis
ἀνα-λύω, loosen up, separate:ἀνά-λυ-σις, separation, analysis
συν-τίθημι (θε), put together:σύν-θε-σις, a putting together, synthesis
σήπω, rot, decay:σῆψις (σῆπ-σις), a rotting, sepsis

αἰσθάνομαι (αἰσθ, αἰσθε), perceive, feel: ἀν-αισθη-σία, insensibility,
   anesthesia
σφύζω (σφυγ), throb, beat: σφυγ-μός, throbbing, pulse.   (Compare
   sphygmo-graph)
βαρβαρίζω (βαρβαριδ), barbarize: βαρβαρισ-μός, barbarism

78. Result nouns are made with the suffix -μaτ. These
are neuter nouns of the consonant declension and drop the
τ in the nominative case, which therefore ends in -μa.

ποιέω, make, compose: ποίη-μα, what is made, or composed, poem
δράω, do, act: δρᾶ-μα, deed, action, drama
γράφω, write: γράμ-μα (γραφ-μα), what is written; in the plural
   (γραμματα), writings, literature, letters (compare Latin litterae).
   From γράμμα come grammar, and the syllable gram in such
   words as monogram, epigram, diagram, program, telegram, etc.
συν-ίστημι (στα), set together: σύ(ν)-στη-μα, what has been set together,
   a system.

79. Denominative nouns are made with the suffix -της
denoting the person concerned with.

πόλι-s, city, state: πολί-της, citizen.   Hence Eng. political, politics
ναῦ-s, ship: ναύ-της, sailor.   Hence syllable naut in argonaut, aeronaut, nautical, nautilus
πατριά, family, clan, tribe: πατριώ-της, clansman, compatriot, (patriot)

80. Quality nouns are made from adjectives with the
suffix -ία.

σοφός, wise: σοφία, wisdom.
φιλόσοφος, wisdom-loving: φ.λοσοφ-ία, love of wisdom, philosophy
πολύ-γαμος, much-married, polygamous: πολυ-γαμ-ία, polygamy

81. Place nouns are made with the suffix -εῖον.

Μοῦσα, Muse: μουσ-εῖον, temple of the Muses, musēum.
Μαύσωλος, Mausolus: Μαυσωλ-εῖον, tomb of Mausolus, mausolēum
ᾠδή, song: ᾠδ-εῖον, place of song, music hall, odēum

Verbal Adjectives

82. It will be observed that some of the suffixes used to form adjectives are the same as those used for forming nouns. Adjectives and nouns were not always clearly distinguished among the Greeks. The fact that they were declined alike, and that adjectives were often used substantively, that is as nouns, tended to obliterate the distinction between them. Thus the adjective "good" in the masculine 'form with the masculine article before it meant "the good man," in the feminine form with the feminine article meant "the good woman," while the neuter meant "the good thing," or "whatever is good," which practice we have carried over into English in the expression "the good, the true, and the beautiful"; that is, "whatever is good, whatever is true, and whatever is beautiful." Generally, however, in English when we place the definite article before an adjective and use it substantively we think of it as plural in a universal or collective sense. When we say "the wise," "the rich," "the young," etc., we mean "all who are wise," etc. The Greeks expressed this by putting the adjective and its article in the plural number, which they indicated by the ending. We cannot make such a distinction in English since the form of the adjective is the same in all genders and numbers.

The practical purpose of this note is to make it clear that many of the forms given in this section, while fundamentally adjectives, may also be used as nouns, and some of them generally appear in English as nouns rather than as adjectives.

83. Adjectives equivalent to *perfect passive participles* are made with the suffix -τος, neuter -τον.

·ρύπτω (κρυφ), *hide, conceal*:κρυπ-τός, *hidden;* English derivatives, crypt, crypto-gram, crypto-gam

δίδωμι (δο), *give*:ἀντί-δο-τον, **antidote**; ἀν-έκ-δο-τον, **anecdote**
ἐπι-τίθημι (θε), *put upon*, *add*:ἐπί-θε-τον, **epithet**
σκέλλω (σκελ-ε), *dry up*:σκελε-τός, *dried up*:σκελε-τόν (σῶμα), *a dried up body, a mummy,* **skeleton**
φύω, *grow*:φυτόν, *something grown, a plant.* Hence English -**phyte** in such words as neophyte (a young plant), **zoöphyte**, **epiphyte**

84. Verbal adjectives denoting *relation, fitness, ability,* or *inclination* are made with the suffix -τικός.

πράσσω (πραγ), *do, accomplish*:πρακ-τικός, *efficient,* **practical**
ἀνα-λύ-ω, *analyze*:ἀνα-λυ-τικός, **analytic, analytical, analytics**
αἰσθάνομαι (αἰσθ-ε), *perceive*:αἰσθη-τικός, *able to perceive,* **aesthetic**; negative **an-aesthetic**
σήπω, *rot, decay*:σηπ-τικός, *productive of decay,* **septic**; negative **a-septic**

85. Many compound adjectives with a verb stem in the second part are made with the suffix -ος. These are also used as agent nouns, and it is in this sense chiefly that they give us English derivatives.

An ε in the verb stem is regularly changed to **o.**

φῶς, genitive φωτ-ός, *light;* φέρω, *bear, carry*:
φωσ-φόρ-ος, *bearing light, light-bearer,* **phosphorus**
γράφω, *write, draw, paint*
*φωτ-ο-γράφ-ος, *light-painter,* **photographer**
γαμέω (γαμ), *marry*:πολύ-γαμ-ος, *much married,* **polygamous**
ἄστρον, *star*:λέγω, *speak, tell about*:
ἀστρο-λόγ-ος, *one who tells about the stars, astronomer,* **astrologer**
βίος, *life*:βιο-γράφ-ος, *life-writer,* **biographer**
μῦθος, *story,* **myth**
μυθο-λόγ-ος, *story-teller; one who tells about the myths,* **mythologist**
ζῷον, *animal*:*ζῳο-λόγ-ος, **zoölogist**

* Greek words marked by an asterisk (*) in this book are either assumed forms, or modern forms, and are not found in Liddell and Scott's *Greek-English Lexicon*. All such words given in this book are formed on the analogy of similar words found in ancient Greek and from words actually found there. They are given because they are the Greek equivalents of English words.

86. It may be noted in passing that from each of these adjectives or agent nouns in -os we may form an abstract noun denoting the state, action, or process, by changing the ending to -ία. (See section 80).

*φωτ-ο-γράφ-ος, *photographer*: *φωτογραφ-ία, *photography*
πολύ-γαμ-ος, *polygamous*: πολυγαμ-ία, *polygamy*
ἀστρο-λόγ-ος, *astrologer*: ἀστρολογ-ία, *astrology*
βιο-γράφ-ος, *biographer*: βιογραφ-ία, *biography*
μυθο-λόγ-ος, *mythologist*: μυθολογ-ία, *mythology*
*ζῳο-λόγ-ος, *zoölogist*: *ζῳολογ-ία, *zoölogy*

The ending -ία is changed to *y* in English. It is through this class of words that we get in English the names of sciences ending in *-ology*.

87. A common mistake is to derive these names of sciences from the noun λόγος, *word*, or *speech*. λόγος is derived from the same root as the last part of these compounds ending in -λογία, and is brother to this ending, not its parent. -λογία does not occur in the Greek language as a separate word, but only in such compounds as μυθο-λογία, ἀστρο-λογία, θεο-λογία, etc., which always presuppose μυθο-λόγ-ος, ἀστρο-λόγ-ος, θεο-λόγ-ος, etc. The -λόγος in the latter part of these and similar words is not the noun λόγος, *speech*, since it means not *speech*, but *speaker*, or rather, *one who speaks about*, and obviously comes directly from the verb λέγω. The identity of form is accidental and this has misled many. The situation is made clear by comparing the similar compounds derived from γράφω, *write*. In this case there is no noun γράφος to cause confusion, and so every one says the latter part of these compounds is from the verb γράφω. The change of ε to ο in the root λεγ of λέγω has also contributed to this confusion. This change, however, is regular and very common. (See sections 72 and 85).

What has just been said will be illustrated and made clearer by the following examples:

*βιο-γράφ-ος, *biographer*:βιο-γραφ-ία, *biography*
γεω-γράφ-ος, *geographer*:γεω-γραφ-ία, *geography*
φωσ-φόρ-ος (φέρω), *light-bearer*:φωσ-φορ-ία, *a bringing of light*
ἀστρο-λόγ-ος, *astrologer*:ἀστρο-λογ-ία, *astrology*
ἀστρο-νόμ-ος (νέμω), *astronomer*:ἀστρο-νομ-ία, *astronomy*
θεο-λόγ-ος (λέγω), *theologian*:θεο-λογ-ία, *theology*

Denominative Adjectives

88. The following suffixes are used to make adjectives from nouns, or rather, from noun stems:

89. -ιο-s, *belonging to, pertaining to.* It appears in English derivatives mostly in adjectives derived from proper names, the Greek ending -ιος being replaced in English by the Latin suffix -ian (-ianus).

Ὄλυμπο-ς, *Olympus*:Ὀλύμπ-ιος, *Olympian*
Κόρινθο-ς, *Corinth*:Κορίνθ-ιος, *Corinthian*
δηλέ-ομαι, *hurt, harm*:δηλη-τήρ, *one who hurts,* or *harms*:δηλη-τήρ-ιος, *hurtful, harmful,* deleterious

90. -κο-s, -ικο-s, denoting *relation, fitness, resemblance,* and corresponding to the ending -τικος in verbals given above (Sec. 84).

πολίτης, *citizen*:πολιτ-ικός, political
ῥήτωρ, *orator*:ῥητορ-ικός, rhetorical
φύσις, *nature*:φυσι-κός, *natural,* physical
καρδία, *heart*:καρδια-κός, *relating to the heart,* cardiac

91. The Greek endings -ικός and -τικός are the source of the common English endings -ic and -tic, the last syllable -os being dropped in English. After the ending -ic, or -tic, in English there is commonly added the ending -al, which is from the Latin suffix -alis. Sometimes we have the English

word ending in *-ic*, sometimes in *-ical*, and in some cases we
can use either.   We can say either poetic or poetical, tragic
or tragical.   We say magnetic, eccentric, graphic, energetic,
enthusiastic.   But we say practical, physical, rhetorical,
theological, etc.   Sometimes the word occurs with both the
endings *-ic* and *-ical*, but the two forms have different meanings, as politic and political.

92. The neuter plural forms of these adjectives were used
in Greek as names for arts and sciences.   The neuter plural
nominative and accusative in all Greek nouns and adjectives
ends in *-a* short.

φυσικά, *matters pertaining to nature, the study of things belonging to
    nature, natural science*, physics
πολιτικά, *things pertaining to the citizens,* or *to the state,* politics
ἦθος, *moral character*:ἠθικά, *things pertaining to moral character,*
    ethics

In these and similar words the English usage imitates the
Greek plural by adding *-s*, the English plural ending.   Hence
we have our names for sciences ending in *-ics*.   A plural
adjective is, however, so foreign to our usage that we forget
that these words are plural, and, as a matter of fact, in our
use of them they are not plural.

We have also names of arts and sciences ending in *-ic*, such
as music, rhetoric, arithmetic, logic.   These correspond to
the Greek practice of using the feminine singular of the adjectives in agreement with the noun τέχνη, *art,* or ἐπιστήμη,
science.   The noun was usually omitted in Greek.   Thus:

μουσική (τέχνη), *musical* (art), music
ἀριθμητική (τέχνη), *the art of counting* or *computation,* arithmetic

The Greeks used either form.   Aristotle has at times
πολιτική (τέχνη, ἐπιστήμη), *political science,* and at times
πολιτικά, politics, in the same sense.

93. -ῖτις, making feminine adjectives. With the feminine noun νόσος, *disease*, understood these adjectives were used as names of diseases.

νέφρος, *kidney*: νεφρ-ῖτις (νόσος), *kidney disease*, **nephritis**
In modern medicine the ending -*itis* signifies *inflammation*
βρόγχια, *bronchial tubes*: *βρογχ-ῖτις, **bronchitis**
ἄρθρον, *joint*: ἀρθρ-ῖτις, *inflammation of joint*, **arthritis**

94. -ης (stem -ες) is used to make both compound adjectives in which the latter part is from a verb stem and compound adjectives in which the latter part is from a neuter noun ending in -ος (stem in -ες. See section 38.).

εὐ-γεν-ής, (from εὖ, *well*, and γεν, stem of γίγνομαι, *be born*), *well-born, noble*. From this we have in English the proper name **Eugene**, and, with a changed ending, **eugenic** and **eugenics**
ὁμο-γενής (from ὁμό-s, *same*, and γένος, *race, kind, genus*), *of the same kind*, **homogeneous**
ἀστερ-ο-ειδής (from ἀστήρ, genitive ἀστέρ-ος, *star*, and εἶδος, stem εἰδες, *appearance, form*), *having the appearance* or *form of a star, like a star*, **asteroid**. This is the origin of our English ending -*oid*, meaning *like*.
ἀνθρωπο-ειδής *having the appearance of a human being*, **anthropoid**
σφαιρο-ειδής, *sphere-like*, **spheroid**
γεω-ειδής contracts to γεώδης, *earth-like*; (**geode**)
σπασμώδης, **spasmodic** from σπασμός, shows a similar ending.

Denominative Verbs

95. These are verbs derived from nouns or adjectives, chiefly from nouns. The most important for our purpose are those ending in -αω, -εω, -οω, -ευω, -αζω, -ιζω.

The only one of these endings appearing in verbs in English is -ιζω, from which comes our common verb ending -*ize*, sometimes changed to -*ise*. We have, however, in English many nouns and adjectives derived from denominative verbs with the other endings given above.

96. The following will illustrate these words and the series
of derivatives which may come from each:

(a) πεῖρα, *trial, attempt, attack*
πειρά-ω, *try, attack*
πειρα-τής, *one who attacks* (ships), **pirate**
πειρα-τικός, **piratical**

(b) ἀριθμός, *number*
ἀριθμέ-ω, *number, count, reckon*
ἀριθμη-τικός, arithmetical: ἀριθμη-τικὴ (τέχνη), **arithmetic**
κόσμος, *order, adornment*
κοσμέ-ω, *set in order, adorn*
κοσμη-τικός, *suited for adorning*, **cosmetic**

(c) νεκρός, *dead; dead body, corpse*
νεκρό-ω, *deaden*
νέκρω-σις, *a deadening*, **necrosis**
σκληρός, *hard*
*σκληρό-ω, *harden*
σκλήρω-σις, *a hardening*, **sclerosis**
*σκληρω-τικός, *hard*, **sclerotic**
νάρκη, *numbness*
ναρκό-ω, *benumb*
νάρκω-σις, *a benumbing*, **narcosis**
ναρκω-τικός, **narcotic**
πῦρ, *fire*
πυρό-ω, *burn*
πύρω-σις, *burning*, **pyrosis**
πύον, *pus*
πυό-ω, *suppurate*
πύω-σις, *suppuration*, **pyosis**

It will be observed from the foregoing illustrations that the
common ending -osis in medical terms comes from this group
of words, that is, from the nouns in -σις from verbs in -οω.

36   EVERYDAY GREEK

(d) φάρμακον, *drug*
φαρμακεύ-ω, *deal in drugs, administer a drug, poison*
φαρμακευ-τικός, pharmaceutic

παῖς, παιδ-ός, *child*
παιδεύ-ω, *bring up a child, educate*
παιδευ-τικός, suited for education, *educative*, paedeutic (paedeutics)
προ-παιδευ-τικός, propaedeutic (propaedeutics)

(e) γυμνός, *naked*
γυμνάζω (γυμναδ), *exercise naked, exercise*
γυμνασ-τής, *one who exercises*, gymnast
γυμνασ-τικός, gymnastic (gymnastics)
γυμνάσ-ιον, *place for exercising*, gymnasium

(f) σοφός, *wise*
σοφίζω, σοφίζομαι (σοφιδ), *act wise, pretend to be wise*
σοφισ-τής, sophist
σοφισ-τικός, sophistic
σόφισ-μα, sophism

ἀγών, *a contest*
ἀγωνίζομαι (ἀγωνιδ), *contend*
ἀντ-αγωνίζομαι, *contend against*, antagonize
ἀντ-αγωνισ-τής, antagonist
ἀντ-αγωνισ-τικός, antagonistic
ἀντ-αγωνισ-μός, antagonism

βάρβαρος, barbarian
βαρβαρίζω, barbarize
βαρβαρισ-μός, barbarism

Ἕλλην, *a Greek*, a Hellene
Ἑλλην-ικός, *Greek*, Hellenic
Ἑλλην-ίζω, Hellenize
Ἑλληνισ-τής, Hellenist (a foreigner who adopted the Greek language and customs)
Ἑλληνισ-τικός, Hellenistic
Ἑλληνισ-μός, Hellenism

97. From this group of words we get our English suffixes *-ize, -ism, -ist, -istic*. These suffixes are now added to many words which are not Greek. Thus Americanize, Americanism, civilize, ritualist, ritualistic.

Compound Words

98. Most of the English words derived from **Greek** are compounds. This is especially true of scientific terms. The principles upon which Greek compounds are formed are, therefore, of especial importance.

NOUNS AND ADJECTIVES

99. Compound nouns and adjectives are closely related in form and in mode of formation and may best be considered together.

100. Three things must be considered in treating of compound nouns and adjectives:

I. The first member of the compound;

II. the second, or last, member of the compound;

III. the meaning of the compound as a whole.

Most of these compounds contain only two words, that is, two stems. If there are more than two stems which enter into a compound, this arises from combining an additional word with a word which is already a compound. When three words are combined in a single compound word one of the words is practically always a preposition, or adverbial prefix.

I. The first member.—If this is a noun or an adjective the stem only is used. If the second member begins with a consonant the first member usually ends in *o*. Stems of the *o*-declension are taken as the norm, or pattern, for the first member of the compounds. A word of the *a*-declension usually changes the final *a* of the stem to *o*, and stems of the consonant declension regularly add an *o*.

Thus o appears as a sort of connecting link at the middle of many compound nouns and adjectives. There are, however, some exceptions in which a noun of the *a*-declension retains its final *a*, or changes it to η.

If the second member of the compound begins with a vowel, a vowel at the end of the first stem is usually dropped.

II. Second, or last, member.—If this begins with a short vowel it is usually lengthened, both *a* and ε becoming η, while o becomes ω.

The endings of the second member, which are the endings of the compound word as a whole, vary, but are generally some of the endings already given above for nouns and adjectives.

Compounds with a verb stem in the second part and with the ending -ος are very common. A verb stem is rarely used in the first part.

III. Meaning of compound nouns and adjectives.—Compound nouns and adjectives may be divided into three classes with reference to their meanings, as follows:

(*a*) *Objective compounds.*—In these the first member stands in the relation of object to the second, either direct or indirect.

στρατό-s, *army;* ἄγω, *lead*
στρατ-ηγ-ός, *army-leader, general;* (strategy, strategic)
γέα (γῆ), *earth, land;* γράφ-ω, *write, write about, describe*
γεω-γράφ-ος, *land-describer,* geographer
ἄστρο-ν, *star;* λέγ-ω, *speak, tell about*
ἀστρο-λόγ-ος, *one who tells about the stars,* astrologer

(*b*) *Descriptive compounds.*—In these the first member describes the second and has the force of an adjective, or adverb, modifying the second member.

μήτηρ, μητρ-ός, *mother;* πόλις, *city*
μητρ-ό-πολις, *mother-city,* metropolis

τῆλε, *far;* σκέπτομαι (σκεπ), *look, see, spy out*
τηλε-σκόπ-ος, *far-seeing, far-looker,* **telescope**
ἀμφι-θέατρον, *double-theater,* **amphitheater**

(*c*) *Possessive compounds.*—These are adjectives. The
first member modifies the second, and the whole compound
means having, or possessing, this modified object. They
may be illustrated by English words like "bright-eyed,"
having bright eyes; "smooth-barked," *having smooth bark,* etc.

μονό-τονος, *having a single tone,* **monotonous**
τρί-πους, τρί-ποδ-ος, *three-footed,* **tripod**
παχύ-δερμ-ος, *thick-skinned,* **pachydermous, pachyderm**
ὁμο-γεν-ής, *of the same kind,* **homogeneous**

COMPOUND VERBS

101. Verbs are not compounded directly with any part of
speech except prepositions. Verbs with prepositions are very
common. The preposition is simply placed at the beginning of the verb without any change except that before a
verb beginning with a vowel the final vowel of a preposition
is usually omitted. If the verb begins with a vowel having
the rough breathing, the breathing combines with a preceding
surd mute and changes it to the corresponding aspirate mute.

βάλλω (βαλ), *throw:*κατα-βάλλω, *throw down* (**catabolism**)
παρα-βάλλω, *throw beside, place beside, compare* (**parable**)
αἱρέω, *take:*δι-αιρέω (διά+αἱρέω), *take apart, separate*
  Compare English **diaeresis,** δι-αίρε-σις
ἀφ-αιρέω (ἀπό+αἱρέω), *take away from* (**aphaeresis**)
λαμβάνω (λαβ, ληβ), *take, seize*
συλ-λαμβάνω (σιν+λαμβάνω), *take together*
συλ-λαβ-ή, *that part of a word taken together, or at one impulse in pronunciation,* a **syllable**
ἐπι-λαμβάνω, *seize upon:*ἐπί-ληψις, *a seizing upon, a fit,* **epilepsy**

SECONDARY COMPOUNDS

102. The classes of compounds described above are what may be termed primary compounds, those which are formed at first hand directly from the constituent stems. From these primary compounds other parts of speech may be formed by changing the suffixes. These may be called secondary compounds. Thus from any one of the compound adjectives and agent nouns described above (see sections **85, 86**) we may form an abstract noun which is the name of the quality, or process, expressed in the adjective, or agent noun. See section **100, III, (a)**.

στρατ-ηγ-ός, general:στρατ-ηγ-ία, generalship, strategy
γεω-γράφ-ος, geographer:γεω-γραφ-ία, geography
ἀστρο-λόγ-ος, astrologer:ἀστρο-λογ-ία, astrology
*ζωο-λόγ-ος, zoölogist:*ζωο-λογ-ία, zoölogy

In these pairs of words the first word in each pair is a primary compound and the second a secondary compound.

103. From these compound nouns and adjectives there are also formed denominative verbs in -έω, -όω, -ίζω.

In classical Greek the denominative verbs from such compounds as are given above nearly all end in -έω, but in our English equivalents we always use the ending -ize, the same as if they ended in -ίζω in Greek.

ἀστρο-λόγ-ος, astrologer:ἀστρο-λογ-έω, astrologize, as if from a Greek form ἀστρο-λογ-ίζω

Notice that we cannot compound the noun ἄστρον and the verb λέγω directly into ἀστρο-λέγω. Such combinations were never made by the ancient Greeks. We must first form the intermediate noun or adjective ἀστρο-λόγ-ος with the ε of the stem of λέγω changed to ο, and then make from this the denominative verb in -έω, ἀστρο-λογ-έω. This is a secondary compound. All

Greek compound verbs in which one part is a noun stem, or an adjective stem, are secondary compounds.

ἀστρο-νόμ-ος, astronomer: ἀστρο-νομ-ία, astronomy
ἀστρο-νομ-έω, rare form ἀστρο-νομ-ίζω, astronomize

NOTE.—The words astrology and astronomy were both in use among the ancient Greeks and meant substantially the same thing. They should really both be translated astronomy. In later times, however, the name astrology came to be used for the pseudo-science of telling the fortunes of men from the stars, while the name astronomy has been retained for the true science of the stars.

ἀστρο-νόμ-ος is from ἄστρο-ν, *star*, and νέμω, *deal out, distribute, arrange, manage*. It probably meant originally one who distributes or arranges the stars, that is, one who studies their arrangement and tries to map it out and describe it.

104. Further examples of secondary compounds:

νέμω, *distribute, manage*: οἶκος, *house, estate, property*
οἰκο-νόμ-ος, *manager of a house or property*, oeconomist
οἰκο-νομ-ία, *management of a house, or an estate, thrift*, economy
οἰκο-νομ-έω, *manage property, exercise thrift*, economize
ὕδωρ, *water* (stem in compounds generally ὑδρο-): φέρω, *carry*
ὑδρο-φόρ-ος, *water-carrier* (hydrophore)
ὑδρο-φορ-έω, *carry water*. There is no corresponding verb in English. There are many of these secondary compound verbs in Greek, but relatively few of them from which we have corresponding verbs in English, although we have English derivatives from many nouns and adjectives from which such verbs are formed in Greek.

IV. WORD GROUPS FOR STUDY

105. Explain the formation of these words and their relation to one another in accordance with the principles given above, pointing out the stem, suffixes, prefixes, and other elements which enter into the formation of each. Give the English words derived from these Greek words, and explain the relations of form and meaning in each instance.

Use a large English dictionary for getting English derivatives and their meanings. The *Century Dictionary* is best for this purpose.

106.
μῦθο-s, *story, legend.*
λέγ-ω, *speak, tell, tell about.*
μυθ-ικός, μυθο-λόγ-ος, μυθο-λογ-ία, μυθο-λογ-ικός, μυθο-λογ-έω.

107.
μορφή, *form, shape.*   μορφό-ω, μόρφω-σις, μορφω-τικός,
μετα-μορφό-ω, μετα-μόρφω-σις, *μετά-μορφ-ος, *μετα-μορφ-ικός,
ἄ-μορφ-ος, πολύ-μορφ-ος, Μορφ-εύς (**morphine**).

108.
μαίνομαι (μαν), *rage, be mad, crazy, be inspired.*
μαν-ία, *μανια-κός, μάν-τις (*sooth-sayer, prophet*),
νεκρο-μαντεία, *χειρ-ο-μαντεία.

109.
μῖμος, *imitator,* mime.
μιμ-ικός, παντ-ό-μιμος, μιμέ-ομαι, μίμη-σις, μιμη-τικός.

110.
ἄρθρο-ν, *joint;* ἀρθρό-ω, ἄρθρω-σις, συν-άρθρω-σις, δι-άρθρω-σις,
ἀρθρ-ῖτις.

III.

τί-θη-μι (θε), *put, place;* θέ-σις, θέ-μα(τ), σύν-θε-σις, συν-θε-τικός,
ἀντί-θε-σις, ἀντι-θε-τικός, ὑπό-θε-σις, ὑπο-θε-τικός, παρ-έν-θε-σις,
*παρ-εν-θε-τικός, διά-θε-σις, *δια-θε-τικός, μετά-θε-σις, ἐπί-θε-τον,
ἐπί-θη-μα(τ), ἐπί-θε-σις, ἀπο-θή-κη, βιβλιο-θή-κη.

112.

ἵστη-μι (στα), *stand, set;* στά-σις, ἔκ-στα-σις, ἐκ-στα-τικός,
στα-τικός, *ὑδρο-στα-τικός, ἀπό-στα-σις, ἀπο-στά-της, σύ(ν)-στη-μα(τ),
συ-στη-ματ-ικός, *συ-στη-ματ-ίζω, διά-στα-σις, δια-στα-τικός, διάστη-μα.

113.

σχίζω (σχιδ), *split;* σχίσ-μα(τ), σχισ-ματ-ικός, σχισ-τός, *σχιστό-
γλωσσος, *σχιστο-γλωσσία, *σχιστό-κυτος.

114.

γέα (old uncontracted form of γῆ), *earth, land;* γεω-γράφ-ος,
γεω-γραφ-ία, *γεω-λόγ-ος, *γεω-λογ-ία, γεω-μέτρης, γεω-μετρ-ία, γεω-
μετρ-ικός, γεω-δαι-σία (δαί-ω), *γεω-δαι-τικός, γεωργός (for γεω-
εργός), γεωργ-ία, γεωργ-ικός.

115.

τάσσω (ταγ), *arrange, station;* τακ-τικός, τακ-τικά, σύν-ταξις,
συν-τακ-τικός.

116.

ἄρχ-ω, *begin, take the lead, command, rule, govern;* ἀρχ-ή,
beginning, rule, government; ἄν-αρχ-ος, ἀν-αρχ-ία, ἱερ-άρχ-ης (ἱερό-ς,
sacred, religious), ἱερ-αρχ-ία, πατρι-άρχ-ης, πατρι-αρχ-ία (πατριά,
tribe, clan, race, those descended from a common father, πατήρ,
genitive πατρ-ός); ἀρχα-ῖος, *of the beginning, ancient;* ἀρχαῖον,
ancient thing, antiquity; ἀρχαῖα, **archives;** ἀρχαιο-λόγ-ος, ἀρχαιο-
λογ-ία, ἀρχα-ικός; τέκτων (τεκτον), *carpenter, builder;* ἀρχι-τέκτων,
ἀρχι-τεκτον-ικός, ἀρχ-άγγελος, ἀρχέ-τυπον, *ἀρχί-βλαστος. This
verbal stem at the beginning of a compound takes the forms ἀρχ-,
ἀρχε-, ἀρχι-. Compare English **arch-bishop, arche-**type, **archi-**
tect.

117.

βάλλω (βαλ, βλη), *throw, place.* παρα-βάλλω, *place beside.* *compare.* παρα-βολή, *comparison,* **parable.** ὑπερ-βάλλω, *throw beyond the mark, go to excess, exaggerate.* ὑπερ-βολ-ή, *exaggeration,* **hyperbole.** προ-βάλλω, *throw before one, propose.* πρό-βλη-μα, *what is thrown before one, a proposition,* **problem.** προ-βλη-ματ-ικός, **problematic.** ἐμ-βάλλω, *insert, inlay.* ἔμ-βλη-μα, *thing inserted, or inlaid,* **emblem.** σύμ-βολ-ον, **symbol.** μετα-βάλλω, *place differently, change, transpose.* μετα-βολ-ή, *change, transposition.* μετα-βολ-ικός, **metabolic.** *μετα-βολίζω, *μετα-βολισ-μός, **metabolism.** κατα-βάλλω, *throw down, destroy.* κατα-βολ-ή, *κατα-βολ-ικός, **catabolic.** *κατα-βολισ-μός, **catabolism.** Contrasted terms are **anabolic, anabolism.**

118.

πάσχω (παθ), *suffer, feel, experience.* πάθος (παθ-ες), *feeling, suffering,* **disease.** παθ-η-τικός, συμ-παθ-ής, συμ-πάθ-εια, συμ-παθ-έω, συμ-παθη-τικός, ἀ-παθ-ής, ἀ-πάθ-εια, *ἀ-παθη-τικός, *παθο-λόγ-ος, *παθο-λογ-ία, παθο-λογ-ικός. Compare **allopathy, homeopathy, osteopathy, pathogenic, pathogenetic.**

119.

φαίνω (φαν), *show, reveal.* φαίν-ομαι, *be shown, show itself,* **appear.** φαιν-όμενον, *that which is shown or appears,* **phenomenon.** φά-σις, *appearance,* **phase.** ἔμ-φα-σις, *a showing in or among,* **emphasis.** ἐμ-φατ-ικός, φαν-ερός, *visible.* *φαν-ερό-γαμ-ος, **phanerogamous, phanerogam.**

φαν-τάζω (φαν-ταδ), *show;* middle and passive, *appear,* often of assumed or unreal appearance. φάντασ-μα, *an appearance,* **phantasm, phantom.** φαν-τασ-ία, *imagination,* **fantasy, fancy.** φαντασ-τικός, **fantastic.** *φαντασμ-αγορία, **phantasmagory.** δια-φαν-ής, *showing through, transparent,* **diaphanous.**

120.

πράσσω (πραγ), *do, accomplish*
πρακ-τικός, *able to accomplish, efficient,* **practical**

πρᾶγ-μα(τ), *deed, thing;* in the plural, *affairs, business*
πραγ-ματ-ικός, *pertaining to things or affairs,* **pragmatic**
πρᾶξις (for πραγ-σις), *doing, practice,* **praxis**

From the stem πραγ-ματ- we also have in English **pragmatize, pragmatism.** and pragmatist, the Greek forms of which would be πραγματ-ίζω, πραγματισμός, πραγματισ-τής, but these do not occur in classical Greek. **Chiropractic** would be χειρο-πρακτικός, from χείρ, *hand,* and πρακτικός.

121.

νέμω, *deal out, distribute, arrange, manage; feed, pasture.* (νέμω and its derivatives show a wide range of meanings in Greek)
νέμ-ε-σις, *a dealing out* (of justice), *divine retribution, righteous indignation,* **nemesis**
ἀστρο-νόμ-ος, *one who studies the distribution of the stars,* **astronomer**
ἀστρο-νομ-ία, **astronomy**
οἶκος, *house, estate, property*
οἰκο-νόμ-ος, *manager of a house, estate, or property*
οἰκο-νομ-ία, *management of house or property, good management, thrift,* **economy**
οἰκο-νομ-ικός, *fitted for management of property,* **economic;** οἰκο-νομ-ικά, **economics**

From the same stem we have in English **economize** and **economist**
ἀγρός, *field, land*
ἀγρο-νόμ-ος, *land-manager, superintendent of public lands*
*ἀγρο-νομ-ία, *management of land,* **agronomy**
*ἀγρο-νομ-ικός, ἀγρο-νομ-ικά, **agronomic, agronomics**
νόμ-ος, *custom, law*
ἀντι-νομ-ία, *opposition to law,* **antinomy**
νομ-ός, *pasture, district,* **nome**
νομάς, νομάδ-ος, *roving about for pasture,* **nomad**
νομαδ-ικός, **nomadic**

122.

φίλος, *friend, lover.* φιλέω, *love.* Prefix φιλο-, *loving*
φιλό-σοφος, *loving wisdom* (σοφία), *lover of wisdom,* **philosopher**
φιλο-σοφία, *love of wisdom,* **philosophy**

φιλο-σοφ-ικός, philosophic

φιλ-άνθρωπος, *lover of mankind*, philanthropist

φιλ-ανθρωπία, *love of mankind*, philanthropy

*φιλ-ανθρωπ-ικός, philanthropic

φιλό-λογος (second part from the noun λόγος, *word, speech,* literature), *loving words, speech, language and literature, a lover of words, language and literature*, philologist

φιλο-λογ-ία, *love of language and literature*, philology

Observe that this differs from the other *-ologies* in the fact that the second part is from the noun λόγος, not from the verb λέγω, and that the verbal element is in the first part, φιλο- (from φιλέω), meaning *loving,* equivalent to a participle of which λόγος is the object, *loving speech, loving literature.*

If the second part of philology were directly from the verb λέγω and had a verbal force and the first part were the noun φίλος, *friend,* it would mean *science of friends,* or *science of friendship.* (See section 87).

"Philology" does not belong in the group of *-ologies,* but in the group of words beginning with the verbal member φιλο-.

φιλο-μαθής, *loving learning* (μάθος), *fond of learning,* philomath

φίλ-ιππος, *fond of horses* (ἵππος), Philipp, Phillip

φιλό-δημος, *loving the people* (δῆμος), philodemic

On the same model we have philharmonic, *fond of harmony or music*

123. To the group of words beginning with **philo-** corresponds a group beginning with **miso-,** *hating.*

μῖσος, τό, *hatred.* μισέω, *hate*

μισ-άνθρωπος, *hating mankind, hater of mankind,* misanthropic, misanthrope

μισ-ανθρωπία, *hatred of mankind,* misanthropy

μισο-γύνης (γύνη, *woman*), *woman-hater,* misogynist

μισό-γυνος, *hating women,* misogynous

μισο-γυνία, *hatred of women,* misogyny

124.

λέγω, *say, speak, tell, tell about*

θεός, *a god, God*

θεο-λόγ-ος, *one who speaks about God,* theologian

θεο-λογ-ία, *speaking about the gods, or God; the science of divine things,* theology
θεο-λογ-ικός, theological
ἀστρο-λόγ-ος, *one who tells about the stars, astronomer,* astrologer
ἀστρο-λογ-ία, *the science of the stars, astronomy,* astrology
ἀστρο-λογ-ικός, *astronomical,* astrological
μῦθος, *story, legend,* myth
μυθο-λόγ-ος, *story-teller; one who tells about the myths,* mythologist
μυθο-λογ-ία, *story-telling,* mythology
μυθο-λογ-ικός, *good at telling stories.* English derivative mythological, with a different shade of meaning
φύσις, *nature*
φυσι-ο-λόγ-ος, *one who tells about nature, a natural philosopher*
φυσι-ο-λογ-ία, *natural philosophy.* English derivative physiology
φυσι-ο-λογ-ικός, physiological
φυσι-ο-λογ-έω, *discourse about nature, tell about natural phenomena.* The corresponding English verb is physiologize, as if from φυσιολογίζω. The English derivatives of this group have a much more restricted meaning than the corresponding Greek words. See next section.

125. The words given in section 124 are all found in ancient Greek authors and are interesting and important as furnishing models for the modern names of sciences ending in *-ology.* Other words of this form occur in ancient writers, but these four groups will serve our purpose here.

The meanings of these words at first were not so technical and specialized as these and similar words have now become. For example, μυθολόγος was simply *a story-teller,* and μυθολογία, *the act or process of telling stories,* not mythology in the modern sense of that term—the whole body of myths, or the scientific study of the myths. Theology was probably the first of these words to take a sense somewhat like that which the word has today. Astrology was used as a synonym for astronomy and may be considered the name of the science such as it was in those times. Physiology was used to signify natural science in general, not in the very restricted sense in which we use the term now.

From the time of Aristotle, however, these words ending in ‑λογία came to be regarded more and more as names of sciences, or systematic bodies of knowledge.

Many of the modern sciences with names ending in *-ology* were entirely unknown to the ancients, but the names we have given them are formed on the analogy of the similar names in use in ancient times and would have been understood by an ancient Greek.

126. If we take as a model the words already given, all we have to do to form similar names for other sciences is to change the first part of the word, to substitute the stem of some other noun in the first part of the compound. In each instance we may have in English as in Greek a group of four words—an abstract noun as name of the science, an agent noun as name of the person who studies the science, a verb, and an adjective. In the evolution of these terms in Greek, however, the name of the person or agent came first, and the abstract name of the science was derived from this. Now we think of the name of the science first and derive the other terms from this.

In English the name of the science ends in *-y* instead of the Greek and Latin *-ia*, and the verb ends in *-ize*, while in Greek it ends in *-έω*. This difference is necessary since *-ize*, Greek ‑ίζω, is the only ending of a Greek verb taken over into English, and so, whatever the ending of the verb may be in Greek, if we use a corresponding verb in English it must end in *-ize* just the same as if the Greek verb ended in -ίζω, as it sometimes does, though not in this group of words. From Greek verbs

in -ίζω are formed agent nouns in -ιστης which is the source of
our English ending -ist. The name of the agent, or scientist,
therefore, regularly ends in -ist in English, occasionally in
-er, while in Greek it ends in -ος.

127. The following examples will serve as illustrations:

ἀστρο-λόγ-ος, astrologer   *γεω-λόγ-ος, geologist
ἀστρο-λογ-ία, astrology   *γεω-λογ-ία, geology
ἀστρο-λογ-ικός, astrological   *γεω-λογ-ικός, geological
ἀστρο-λογ-έω, astrologize   *γεω-λογ-έω, geologize

The following are given in English form only and in the
English order:

Biology, biologist, biological, (biologize)
Zoölogy, zoölogist, zoölogical, (zoölogize)
Physiology, physiologist, physiological, physiologize
Psychology, psychologist, psychological, psychologize

The verb in this class of words is not very common in
English. In many cases it is not in use at all. "Zoölogize"
is not given in the *Century Dictionary*. "Biologize" is rare
and used in the sense of mesmerize. "Physiologize" is used
chiefly in the old Greek sense of *speculate concerning nature*.

128. All the additional knowledge needed for other words
of this type is to know what the first part of the compound
comes from. Following is a list of nouns so used. Give the
group of English words derived from each of these corresponding to the groups given above.

ἄνθρωπος, *man, mankind*   δένδρον, *tree*
αἴτιον, *cause*   κόγχη, *shell-fish, shell*
ψυχή, *soul, mind*   ἰχθύ-s, *fish*
ἰστός, *web, tissue*   ὄρνις, ὄρνιθ-ος, *bird*
νεῦρον, *sinew, nerve*   ἔμβρυο-ν, *foetus, embryo*

τέλος, τέλε-ος, *end, purpose*
βακτήριο-ν, *a little staff,* bacterium
πάθος, the way a person is affected, *feeling, suffering, disease*
ἔτυμος, *true*:neut. ἔτυμον, *true literal meaning of a word*

according to its origin; also *root of a word*
οὖς, ὠτ-ός, *ear*
ῥίς, ῥιν-ός, *nose*
ὀφθαλμός, *eye*
γυνή, γυναικ-ός, *woman*
σεισμός, *earthquake*

129. From λέγω, *say, speak,* come also the following words:

λόγος, *word, speech, reason, proportion, prose*
λογο-γράφ-ος, *speech-writer, prose-writer,* logographer
λογο-γραφ-ία, *speech-writing, prose-writing,* logography
λογ-ικός, *reasonable, rational,* logical
λογ-ική, logic
ἀνά-λογος, *according to a fixed proportion, proportional,* analogous
λέξις (for λέγ-σις), *a speaking, speech, word*
λεξι-κόν (βιβλίον), *word-book,* lexicon
δια-λέγ-ομαι, *converse*
δια-λεκ-τικός, *conversational,* dialectic
διά-λεκ-τος, *conversation, style of speaking,* dialect
διά-λογος, *conversation,* dialogue
πρό-λογος, *fore-word,* prologue
ἐπί-λογος, *after-speech,* epilogue
εὐ-λογ-ία, *well-speaking, praise,* eulogy; we also have eulogize, eulogist, and eulogistic

130.
λέγω, *pick, gather*
ἐκ-λεκ-τικός, *inclined to pick out* or *select,* eclectic
συλ-λέγω (συν+λέγω), *gather together, collect*
συλ-λογ-ή, *a collection* (of poems, etc.), sylloge
ἐκ-λογ-ή, *a picking out, selection,* eclogue

131.
κράτος, τό, *might, power, rule*:κρατέω, *exercise power, rule*
δῆμος, *people, common people*

ₖημο-κρατ-ία, *rule by the people,* **democracy**

δημο-κρατ-ικός, **democratic;** as a noun, **democrat**

In the same way we have from ἄριστος, *best,* **aristocracy, aristocratic,** and **aristocrat**

From αὐτός, *self,* we get **autocracy, autocratic,** and **autocrat**

From πλοῦτος, *wealth,* we get **plutocracy, plutocratic,** and **plutocrat**

From ὄχλος, *crowd, mob,* we get **ochlocracy,** etc. I once heard a distinguished scholar use very effectively the expressive word **cleptocratic,** from κλέπτης, *thief,* although "cleptocratic" is not in the English dictionary.

132.

δοκέω (δοκ), *think, seem, seem good, seem best*

δόγ-μα(τ), *what seems best, one's opinion* or *conviction of what is right and good,* **dogma**

The dogma of a governing body in state or church is its decree. A law, ordinance or decree passed by the Athenian assembly began regularly with the words ἔδοξε τῇ βουλῇ καὶ τῷ δήμῳ, "*It seemed best to the senate and the popular assembly,*" equivalent to our enacting clause: "Be it enacted by the senate and general assembly." The decree itself was called a δόγμα—what seemed best to the governing body.

δόξα, *opinion, reputation, honor, glory*

δοξο-λογ-ία, *the expression of glory to God,* **doxology,** as in the well-known doxology: "Glory (δόξα) be to the Father, to the Son, and to the Holy Ghost"

παρά-δοξος, *contrary to opinion* or *expectation,* **paradoxical;** as a noun, **paradox**

ὀρθός, *upright, straight, right*

ὀρθό-δοξος, *having right opinion,* **orthodox**

ἕτερος, *other* (of two), *different, wrong*

ἑτερό-δοξος, *of other opinion, of wrong opinion,* **heterodox**

ὀρθο-δοξία, **orthodoxy.** ἑτερο-δοξία, **heterodoxy**

133.

ἄγω (ἀγ, reduplicated stem ἀγαγ), *lead*

δημ-αγωγ-ός, *leader of the people* (generally in a bad sense, *one who misleads the people*), **demagogue.**

δημ-αγωγ-ία, demagogy
δημ-αγωγ-ικός, demagogical
παῖς, παιδ-ός, child, boy
παιδ-αγωγ-ός, boy-leader, pedagogue
παιδ-αγωγ-ία, pedagogy
παιδ-αγωγ-ικός, pedagogical
στρατός, army
στρατ-ηγ-ός, army-leader, general
στρατ-ηγ-ία, generalship, strategy
στρατ-ηγ-ικός, strategic
στρατ-ηγ-έω, be a general
στρατ-ήγη-μα, an act of generalship, stratagem

134. ὕδωρ, ὕδατ-ος (stem in compounds takes the form ὑδρο- before consonants, ὑδρ- before vowels), water.

αὐλός, pipe
ὑδρ-αυλ-ικός, pertaining to water-pipes, hydraulic

NOTE.—αὐλός is a pipe in the sense of a musical instrument. The term "hydraulic" has probably come into scientific language from the Greek ὕδραυλις, a sort of musical instrument with pipes made to sound by means of moving water, a water organ, also called ὑδραυλικὸν ὄργανον. It was invented by Ctesibius, a Greek who lived at Alexandria in Egypt. See Athenaeus 174.

ἵστημι (στα), set, stand
*ὑδρο-στα-τικός, having to do with the standing of water, hydrostatic, hydrostatics
φοβέομαι, fear
ὑδρο-φόβ-ος, water-fearing: ὑδρο-φοβ-ία, fear of water, hydrophobia
ὕδρα, a water-snake, hydra

In Greek mythology the Lernaean Hydra was a monster with nine heads, each of which when cut off was replaced by two. The monster was slain by Hercules, who cut off the heads and cauterized the wounds so that they could not sprout new heads.

The stem ὑδρ- with the ending -ant, of Latin origin, gives hydrant. With the suffix -ate we get hydrate.

There is a very large number of technical and scientific terms beginning with **hydro-**, or **hydr-**. They can be found in any large English dictionary.

135.

ἔρδω (ἐργ), *work*

ἐν-εργ-ής, *at work, active*

ἐν-έργ-εια, *activity,* **energy**

ἐν-εργ-έω, *be at work, be active*

ἐν-εργη-τικός, *able to be at work, inclined to work,* **energetic**

μέταλλον, *a mine;* later, a metal

μεταλλουργός (μεταλλο-εργός), *mine-worker, metal-worker*

μεταλλουργ-ία, *mine-working, metal-working,* metallurgy

χειρουργός (χειρ-ο-εργ-ός), *hand-worker,* **surgeon**

χειρουργ-ία, *hand-work,* surgery, chirurgery

χειρουργ-ικός, **surgical, chirurgical**

ἀ-εργ-ός, contracted form ἀργός, *not working, idle;* hence **argon**

ὄργ-ανον, *thing to work with, tool, instrument,* organ

From the word organ with the usual suffixes we form **organic, organize, organism, organist**

NOTE.—The word ὄργανον had in Greek about the same range of meanings as its English derivative organ. The musical instrument called a water-pipe organ, ὑδραυλικὸν ὄργανον, has already been referred to above (see section 134, note). From this in course of time was evolved the church organ. The word was also used by the ancients for an organ of the body, such as the eye.

ἔργον, *work;* (**ergograph**)

136. Changes in the meaning of words.—It must have been observed already by the student of this book that in many of the English words derived from Greek the meaning of the English word corresponds only in part to that of the Greek word from which it is derived, and that sometimes the connection is rather remote. The meaning of words changes with their use and with changing ideas and processes. The history of words and their changes in meaning and application is, to a large extent, a history of civilization, of the intellectual and moral development of the people who used these words.

There are various ways in which the meanings of words change. Sometimes the meaning is *generalized* and becomes broader; sometimes it is *specialized* and restricted to a part of what it originally covered. New ideas are usually expressed by using old words in a new sense. Often the name is given to a new discovery in a more or less arbitrary way. If the name is made from a Greek word, or from two or more Greek words, the namer tries to use Greek words which express something more or less characteristic of the thing he is naming. Sometimes the name is based upon a misapprehension or false conception, and while the name sticks the etymological meaning becomes inappropriate when the facts are better understood. The word, however, serves its purpose by taking on a new meaning.

The English words of Greek origin may be divided historically into two classes.

The first class includes those words which were used by the ancient Greeks themselves in approximately the same sense in which we now use them, and which have been in use more or less continuously by scholars from ancient times to the present. These constitute the basis of all our Greek terms in English, and furnish the models upon which the later scientific and philosophical terms have been formed. The words of this first class have come into our language along with the ideas which they express, both the thing designated and its name being of Greek origin. Such words are **poetry, drama, epic, theater, history, philosophy, theology, mythology, astronomy, mathematics, politics, democracy, physics, geometry, organ, energy, analysis, synthesis,** and many others. These words, too, have changed in meaning with increasing knowledge and changing ideas, but the change has been a gradual growth.

The second clas consists of words introduced in modern times as names of new inventions and discoveries, or new ideas of any kind which required new names. Examples of such words are **telegraph, telephone, photograph, protoplasm, phagocyte, microbe,** and indeed most of our modern scientific terms of G.·eek origin.

Etymologically **physics** and **physiology,** both of which are derived from the Greek word φύσις, *nature,* mean the same thing, *science of nature,* or *natural science* in general. Both these words were used in this general sense by Aristotle and other ancient Greek writers, and apparently without any distinction in meaning. Each of these terms has now become restricted to a special division of natural science.

On the other hand **economy,** which originally meant the management of a house and its belongings, has been broadened out to include much more. It had acquired much of this broader meaning already in ancient times. The same may be said of the related words, "economic," "economics," and "economical."

Geometry was at first merely the measurement of land, but it came very early to have a much broader meaning and application.

On the whole, however, the instances in which a word has been restricted in its meaning to a part of the ground originally covered by it are much more numerous than those in which it has become more general in its meaning, and this is especially true of scientific terms.

In modern scientific terms Greek words are often used in a specialized technical sense which was entirely unknown to the ancient Greeks. Thus the Greek word κύτος which meant a *bowl, vase,* or *jar,* or anything shaped like them, has been adopted in modern science to designate a *cell,* a thing of which the ancient scientists had no knowledge. The word νεῦρον used in scientific language to designate *nerve* had the meaning *sinew* or *tendon* in ancient Greek. It was first used in the modern sense of nerve by the physician Galen in the second century after Christ. The Greek word ἤλεκτρον meaning *amber,* or *an amber-colored metal,* is used in modern science to designate *electricity.* Many other similar illustrations might be given but these will be sufficient here. There are naturally no words for things hitherto unknown and the best that can be done in making a new name for a new discovery is to take an old word which designated something partially like the new idea and give this old word a changed meaning.

137. The older generation of scientists were, for the most part, also Greek scholars and made their scientific terms conform in the main to the genius and rules of the Greek language. In recent years with the rapid growth of scientific discovery and with intense specialization there has come into use a flood of new scientific terms formed from Greek words, and it was inevitable that some of these should be clumsily formed and impossible of explanation in accordance with the principles and usages of the Greek language. Still it is true of these words that they may be understood and remembered much better by knowing the Greek words from which they are formed.

138. Scientific terms are now so numerous and for the most part so highly technical that they cannot to any considerable extent be included in a manual like the present one, but each student must specialize upon those which he needs for his own special field of study. The general knowledge given in this handbook should assist him greatly in learning the derivation and meaning of the special terms belonging to his own specialty.

139. Attention may here be called to a class of words spoken of by etymologists as corruptions. When a word of classical origin came to be used not merely by scholars and educated people, but also by the illiterate masses, changes were brought about by mistaken or careless pronunciation, and a word might change little by little until its original source could scarcely be recognized. In such cases we can usually find intermediate forms preserved in books of different dates and places by means of which the later corrupted form can be traced back to its original source.

Examples of such words are, bishop, from the Greek ἐπίσκοπ-ος, overseer; devil, from the Greek διάβολος; surgeon, from the Greek χειρουργός; priest, from πρεσβύτερος. The intermediate forms may be seen in any large English dictionary under the English words.

140. Metaphysics, μετὰ φυσικά, after physics. This term was first applied in Roman times to a group of treatises which came after the Physics (μετὰ φυσικά) in the collected works of Aristotle. Later the origin of the title was forgotten and it was supposed to describe the subject-matter of these treatises. From Aristotle's works the term was transferred to other discussions of a similar character and finally became the name for a branch of philosophy. Aristotle did not give this name to his work, and the term has no special significance except as it acquired it in later times.

141. Following are a few groups of English words of Greek derivation arranged so far as practicable by departments of thought and endeavor. None of the groups is complete, and some of the words might with equal reason be placed in other groups. The first word in each group will be suggestive

of the nature of the group. The plan has been to get typical words in each group and to present both some common words and some highly technical terms.

The student should use these words as material for practice in tracing derivations. It is hoped that with the help of the principles and illustrations already given he may be able to think out many of these derivations without looking up the words in a dictionary. After trying what he can do unaided he may resort to the index and vocabulary at the end of this book, and finally to some large English dictionary. The *Century Dictionary* is one of the best for words of Greek origin.

Additional words for study may be found in the index.

1. gymnastics
gymnasium
athlete
athletic
acrobat
trophy

2. music
melody
harmony
tone
tune
monotone
meter
chorus
chord
symphony
antiphony
anthem
psalm

doxology
organ
metronome

3. politics
policy
political
economic
ethnic
aristocracy
autocracy
oligarchy
monarchy
tyranny
despotism
dynasty
democracy
democratic
plutocracy
anarchy

patriot
hero
cosmopolitan
monopoly
emporium
epoch
ostracize

4. mathematics
arithmetic
geometry
trigonometry
analytics
cone
cube
sphere
cylinder
prism
pentagon
polygon

diameter
perimeter
diagonal
base
center
hypotenuse
parallel
diagram
problem
axiom
theorem
scholium

5. physics
dynamics
mechanics
optics
acoustics
hydraulics
hydrostatics
eccentric
electric
elastic
telegraph
telegram
telephone
pneumatic
electrolysis
magnetic
thermodynam-
ics
stereopticon

6. botany
ecology

taxonomy
protoplasm
cytoplasm
stigma
anther
petal
calyx
cryptogam
phanerogam
spore
endogen
exogen
angiosperm
gymnosperm
chlorophyl
perianth
parasite
epiphyte
geotropism
heliotropism

7. philosophy
psychology
psychic
logic
ethics
stoic
skeptic
pragmatic
scholastic
category
idea
ideal
idealism
hypnosis

hypnotic
ergograph

8. zoölogy
ichthyology
ornithology
embryology
entomology
protozoön
metabolism
xiphoid
azygos
entomostraca
malacostraca
aptera
diptera
ctenophora
coelenterata
arthropoda
xiphosura
notochord
coelomata
chaetognatha

9. poetry
poet
poem
epic
lyric
drama
dramatic
tragedy
tragic
comedy
comic

bucolic
elegy
epigram
idyl
theater
scene
melodrama
prologue
episode
epilogue
rhythm
ode
threnody
strophe
antistrophe
dactyl
anapest

10. rhetoric
theme
thesis
topic
epitome
apothegm
emphasis
apostrophe
metaphor
trope
phrase
paraphrase
paragraph
parenthetic
period
graphic
laconic

idiom
dialogue
apology
comma
colon
hyphen
dieresis
synonym
anonymous
pseudonym
sarcasm

11. ecclesiastic
Catholic
Presbyterian
Methodist
Episcopalian
Christ
apostle
evangelist
bishop
presbyter
deacon
cathedral
diocese
synagogue
ascetic
hermit (eremite)
priest
monk
heresy
heretic
agnostic
schism
alms

eleëmosynary
apostasy
prophet
liturgy
anthropomor-
phism
theism
atheism
pantheism
mystic
idol
idolatry
theology
theosophy
cemetery
epitaph
cenotaph
angel
hierarchy
demon
devil

12. physician
anatomy
physiology
neurology
hygiene
anodyne
epidermis
hypodermic
symptom
diet
nausea
chronic
anesthetic

anaemia
epidemic
osmosis
ptomaine
antitoxin
therapeutic
pediatry
prophylaxis
atrophy
hypertrophy
microbe
bacteria
cytogenesis
cytoblast

phagocyte
(should be
cytophag)
sepsis
antiseptic
symphysis
synarthrosis
synchondrosis
cyst
myelocyst
poliomyelitis
gastritis
pericardium
peritoneum

clinic
sphygmograph
hemorrhage
neurosis
neurotic
neuritis
neurocyte
neuriatry
cystectomy
chondroid
hypochondriac
psychiatry

142. The following list contains some names of men and women. Look up the Greek words in the vocabulary.

Alexander, from ἀλέξω and ἀνήρ
Bernice, Βερενίκη=Φερενίκη, from φέρω and νίκη
Catharine, or Catherine, from καθαρός
Christopher, Χριστοφόρος, Χριστός, φέρω
Cora, from κόρη, κόρα
Dorothea, Dorothy, from δῶρον and θεός
Eugene, Εὐγενής, from εὖ and γίγνομαι (γεν)
Eunice, from εὖ and νίκη
George, Γεώργιος, from γεωργός
Georgia, Γεωργία, feminine of Γεώργιος
Helen, Ἑλένη, a prominent character in the Homeric poems
Homer, Ὅμηρος, reputed author of the *Iliad* and the *Odyssey*
Ida, Ἴδη and Ἴδα, ἴδη and ἴδα
Irene, from εἰρήνη
Iris, Ἶρις, ἴρις
Leon, λέων
Margaret, μαργαρίτης

Melissa, μέλισσα

Myron, Μύρων, name of a famous Greek sculptor

Nicholas, Νικόλāος, from νίκη and λāός

Peter, πέτρος

Phoebe, Phebe, from φοῖβος, feminine φοίβη

Philip, Phillip, φίλιππος, from φίλος and ἵππος

Phyllis, from φύλλον

Sophia, σοφία

Stephen, Steven, from στέφανος

Theodore, from θεός and δῶρον

Theophilus, from θεός and φίλος

V. VOCABULARY

143. In this vocabulary if the stem of a verb is not obvious it is added in parentheses after the verb. Greek words in parentheses after other words in the vocabulary are intended to suggest the derivation of the Greek word which they follow. These words in parentheses may be found defined in their proper places in the vocabulary.

Not all the meanings of the Greek words are given in this vocabulary, but only those meanings which are helpful in tracing the derivation of English words. Quite often it is the rarer meaning of a Greek word which appears in its English derivative; especially so in scientific terms.

The meanings are given in such an order as to lead up to the meanings of the English derivatives. Very often none of the meanings of the Greek word are exactly the same as that of its English derivative, or derivatives, and the meanings given for Greek words in this vocabulary must not be taken as definitions of the English derivative which is usually given at the end of the list of meanings. To get the exact significance of the English word as used at the present time the English dictionary should be consulted. In the case of medical and other scientific terms a special dictionary, such as *Stedman's Medical Dictionary*, may be consulted.

A

ἀ- before consonants, ἀν- before vowels. Negative prefix like un- in English: *not, without.*

ἀγγεῖον: *vessel, vase, jar.*

ἄγγελος: *messenger,* **angel.**

ἀ-γνωσ-τικός (γιγνώσκω): *unable to know,* **agnostic.**

*ἀγρο-νομ-ία: *management of land,* **agronomy.**

ἀγρο-νόμ-ος: *manager of land, superintendent of lands.*

ἀγρός: *field, land, country.*

ἄγω (ἀγ, ἀγαγ, reduplicated stem): *lead.*

ἀγών: *contest, trial.*

ἀγωνία: *struggle, anguish,* agony.

ἀγωνίζομαι (ἀγωνιδ): *contend, struggle.*

ἀδελφός, ἀδελφή: *brother, sister.*

ἄ-ζυγος (ζύγον): *without a yoke, unyoked.*

ἀήρ, gen. ἀέρ-ος: air.

ἀθλέω: *contend for a prize* in feats of strength and skill, especially in the public games.

ἀθλη-τής: *contestant in the games,* athlete.

ἆθλον: *prize in the games.*

αἰθήρ: *the clear upper air,* aether.

αἷμα, gen. αἷματ-ος: *blood.*

αἱμορ-ραγ-ία, from αἷμα+ῥήγ-νυμι (ῥαγ): *bursting forth of the blood,* hemorrhage.

αἴνιγμα, gen. αἰνίγματ-ος: *dark saying, riddle,* enigma.

αἰνίσσομαι (αἰνιγ): *speak in riddles, hint.*

αἵρε-σις: *a choosing, choice, sect,* heresy.

αἱρε-τικός: *sectarian,* heretic.

αἱρέω, mid. αἱρέομαι: *take,* mid. *choose.*

αἰσθάνομαι (αἰσθ, αἰσθε): *perceive.*

αἴσθη-σις: *perception.*

αἰσθη-τικός: *able to perceive, good at perceiving,* aesthetic.

αἰτιο-λογ-ία (from αἴτιον+λεγω): *discussion of causes,* aetiology.

αἴτιον: *cause, reason.*

ἀκέομαι: *heal, cure.*

ἀκμή: *point, highest point, prime,* acme.

ἀκρο-βα-τής, from ἄκρος+βαίνω (βα): *one who goes highest, high-goer,* acrobat.

ἄκρος: *highest, topmost.*

ἀκουσ-τικός: *pertaining to hearing,* acoustic.

ἀκούω: *hear.*

ἀλγέω: *feel pain, suffer, grieve.*

ἄλγος (stem ἀλγες): *pain, suffering.*

ἀλέξω (ἀλεξ, ἀλεξε): *ward off.*

ἀλλήλοιν: *of one another, to or for one another.*

ἄλλος: *other, another.*

ἀ-μέθυσ-τος, verbal adjective of μεθύω with neg. prefix: *not drunken;* ἀ-μέθυστος λίθος, *the stone which prevents drunkenness,* amethyst.

ἀμοιβή: *exchange, requital, recompense.*

ἄ-μορφος: *formless, shapeless,* amorphous.

ἀμφί: *about, on both sides.*

ἀμφι-θέατρον: *double theater,* amphitheater.

ἀνά: *up;* in composition sometimes *back, again.*

ἀνα-βάλλω (βαλ): *throw up, build up.*

ἀνα-βολή: *what is thrown up, or built up, a mound.*

*ἀνα-βολικός: *building up, constructive,* anabolic.

*ἀνα-βολισμός: *upbuilding, constructive metabolism.*

NOTE.—The last word is purely modern and the meanings given for the three preceding words have been selected so as to lead up to this modern derivative, anabolism.

ἀν-αισθησία (αἰσθάνομαι): *insensibility,* anesthesia.

*ἀν-αισθη-τικός: anesthetic.

ἀν-αίσθη-τος: *without sense or feeling, insensate.*

ἀν-αλγη-σία: *freedom from pain, insensibility,* analgesia.

ἀνά-λογος: *according to proportion, comparable,* analogous.

ἀνά-λυ-σις: *a loosing up, separation into parts,* analysis.

ἀνα-λυ-τικός: *pertaining to analysis,* analytic.

ἀνα-λύω: *loosen up, dissolve,* analyze.

ἀν-αρχία: *absence of rule or government,* anarchy.

ἄν-αρχος: *without ruler or government,* anarchical.

ἀνα-τέμνω (τεμ): *cut up, dissect.*

ἀνα-τομ-ή: *dissection,* anatomy.

ἄνεμος: *wind.*

ἀνεμώνη: *wind flower,* anemone.

ἀνήρ, gen. ἀνδρ-ός: *man, male human being.*

ἄνθεμον (longer form of ἄνθος): *flower.*

ἄνθος (ἄνθες): *flower, blossom.*

ἄνθρωπος: *man, mankind, human being* (either male or female).

ἀντ-αγωνίζομαι: *contend against,* antagonize.

*ἀντ-αγωνισμός: antagonism.

ἀντ-αγωνιστής: antagonist.

*ἀντ-αγωνιστικός: antagonistic.

ἀντί: *against, opposite.*

ἀντί-θε-σις: *a putting opposite, what is put opposite,* antithesis.

ἀντι-θετικός: *put in opposition,* antithetic.

*ἀντι-νομία: *opposition to law,* antinomy.

ἀντί-φωνος: *sounding opposite, or in response, responsive;* in neut. ἀντίφωνον, *responsive singing,* antiphony, anthem.

ἀν-ώδυνος, -ον (ὀδύνη): *without pain, allaying pain;* ἀνώδυνον <φάρμακον>, *a drug alleviating pain,* anodyne.

ἀν-ωμαλία (ἀνώμαλος): *unevenness, irregularity,* anomaly.

ἀν-ώμαλος (ὁμαλός): *uneven, out of level,* anomalous.

ἀξίωμα: *that which is demanded as a basis for reasoning, that which is assumed as self-evident,* axiom.

ἄξων: *axle, axis.*

ἀορτή (from ἀείρω, stem ἀερ, *lift-up*): aorta.

ἀ-πάθεια (πάσχω, παθ): *lack of feeling, insensibility,* apathy.

*ἀ-παθητικός: *without feeling or sensibility;* apathetic.

ἀπό: *from, away from.*

ἀπο-θήκη: *a place in which to put things away, a store-house,* apothecary.

ἀπολογέομαι: *speak in one's defense, defend one's self.*

ἀπολογητικός: *inclined to defend one's self, of the nature of a defense,* apologetic.

ἀπολογία: *defense by speech,* apology.

ἀπό-στα-σις (ἵστημι, στα): *a standing away from, withdrawal, desertion,* apostasy.

ἀπο-στά-της: *one who deserts, a run-away slave, an* apostate.

ἀπό-στολος (ἀπο-στέλλω): *one who is sent away on a mission, a messenger, envoy, ambassador;* in the New Testament, *a missionary, an* apostle.

ἀπο-στρέφω: *turn away from.*

ἀπο-στροφή: *a turning away, that is, from all others to address one specially, an* apostrophe.

ἀπο-φθέγγομαι: *speak out plainly and to the point.*

ἀπό-φθεγμα: *a terse pointed saying,* an apophthegm.

ἄ-πτερος (πτέρον): *without wings,* wingless.

ἀράχνη: *a spider.*

ἀργός (contracted from ἀ-εργός): *not working, inactive, idle.*

ἀρθρ-ῖτις: *inflammation of a joint,* arthritis.

ἄρθρον: *joint.*

ἀρθρόω: *make a joint, unite by means of a joint, articulate.*

ἄρθρω-σις: *union by means of a joint,* arthrosis.

ἀριθμέω: *count, number, reckon up.*

ἀριθμη-τικός: *pertaining to counting or reckoning,* arithmetical.

ἀριθμητική <τέχνη>: *art of counting and reckoning,* arithmetic.

ἀριθμός: *number.*

ἄριστος: *best.*

ἄρκτος: *a bear, a constellation in the northern heavens, the north.* Hence ἀρκτικός, *northern,* arctic.

ἀρμονία: *a fitting together,* harmony.

ἀρτηρία: *windpipe,* artery.

ἀρχ-άγγελος: *chief messenger,* archangel.

ἀρχαῖα (neut. plur. of ἀρχαῖος): *ancient things, antiquities,* archives.

ἀρχαϊκός: *old-fashioned, primitive,* archaic.

ἀρχαιο-λογία: *account of ancient things,* archaeology.

ἀρχαιο-λόγ-ος: *one who tells about ancient things, an antiquarian.*

ἀρχαῖος: *belonging to the beginning, ancient.*

ἀρχέ-τυπον: *first type,* archetype

ἀρχή: *beginning, leadership, rule, government.*

*ἀρχί-βλαστος: *the initial sprout or germ,* archiblast.

ἀρχι-τεκτον-ικός: *pertaining to the master-builder,* architectonic.

ἀρχι-τέκτων: *master-builder,* architect.

ἄρχω: *begin, be first; lead, command, rule.*

ἄ-σβεστος (σβέννυμι): *unquenchable;* later, *unburnable,* asbestos.

ἀ-σθενής (σθένος): *without strength, weak, sick,* asthenic.

ἀ-σθένεια: *weakness, sickness,* asthenia.

ἄσθμα: *shortness of breath, panting, difficulty in breathing,* asthma.

ἀσκέω: *exercise, train, discipline.*

ἀσκη-τικός: *suited for discipline,* ascetic.

ἀστερο-ειδής: *having the form or appearance of a star,* asteroid.

ἀστήρ, gen. ἀστέρ-ος: *star.*

ἀστρο-λογ-ία: *astronomy,* astrology.

ἀστρο-λόγ-ος: *one who tells about the stars, astronomer,* astrologer.

ἄστρον (another form of ἀστήρ): *star.*

ἀστρο-νομ-ία: *arrangement and distribution of the stars,* astronomy. See νέμω.

ἀστρο-νόμ-ος: *one who studies the distribution or arrangement of the stars, an* astronomer.

ἄ-συλος (συλάω): *safe from violence, inviolate;* ἄσυλον ἱερόν: *an inviolable shrine, a refuge, an* asylum.

ἀτμός: *steam, vapor*

ἄ-τομ-ος (τέμνω): *uncut, indivisible;* ἄτομον, *an indivisible particle,* atom.

ἀ-τροφία (τρέφω): *lack of nutrition,* atrophy.

ἄ-τροφος: *without nourishment.*

αὐθ-έντης (αὐτός+ἕντης, *doer*): *self-doer, real author.*

αὐθεντικός: *belonging to the real author,* authentic.

αὐλός: *a pipe* (a musical instrument somewhat like a clarinet).

*αὐτο-ματ-ικός: *like an automaton,* automatic.

αὐτό-μα-τος (root μα, *desire, wish, will*): *self-willed, self-impelled, acting of one's own accord;* neut. αὐτόματον: *a thing which acts of its own accord, an* automaton.

αὐτός: *self, himself, herself, itself.*

αὐτ-οψία: *a seeing it one's self,* autopsy.

ἀφαίρεσις (ἀπό+αἱρέω): *a taking away,* apheresis.

ἀφαιρέω: *take away.*

B

βαίνω (βα): *step, stand, walk, go.*

βακτήριον, plur. βακτήρια: *a little staff, a little cane;* bacterium, bacteria.

βάλλω (βαλ, βλη): *throw, cast, put.*

βαρβαρίζω: *behave like a barbarian.*

βαρβαρισμός: barbarism.

68 EVERYDAY GREEK

βάρβαρος: barbarous, a barbarian.

βάρος: weight.

βαρύς: heavy.

βαρύ-τονος: heavy-toned, barytone.

βάσις (βαίνω): a stepping, standing, that on which anything stands, pedestal, basis, base.

βιβλιο-θήκη (τίθημι): book-case, library.

βιβλίον: book; τὰ βιβλία: the books, the Bible.

βίος: life, especially, course of life, life history.

βλαστός: sprout, shoot, germ.

Βορέας: north wind, the north, Boreas.

βοτάνη: grass, fodder, vegetation.

βουκολικός: pertaining to cattle-herdsmen, bucolic.

βου-κόλος: cowherd, herdsman.

βοῦς (stem βου): cow, ox; in plur., cattle.

βού-τυρον (τυρός): butter.

βραχίων: upper arm (between shoulder and elbow).

βρόγχια(plural): bronchial tubes.

*βρογχ-ῖτις: bronchitis.

βρόγχος: windpipe, trachea.

Γ

γάλα, gen. γάλακτ-ος: milk.

γαλαξίας: Milky Way, galaxy.

γαμέω (γαμ): marry.

γαστήρ, gen. γαστρ-ός: stomach, belly.

γαστρ-ικός: relating to the stomach, gastric.

γέα, contracted form, γῆ: earth, land.

NOTE.—The old uncontracted form γέα was generally used in the first part of a compound word, the final -α changing to -ω, so that the stem assumes the form γεω-, as in γεω-γραφία.

γενεά (γίγνομαι): race, stock, family.

γενεα-λογία: an account of one's pedigree, genealogy.

γένε-σις (γίγνομαι): becoming, origin, creation, genesis.

γένος (stem γενες): race, kind, genus (Latin equivalent).

γεράνιον: name of a plant, crane-bill, geranium.

γέρανος: a crane.

γεω-γράφ-ος: one who writes about the earth, a geographer.

γεω-δαισία (δαίω): a dividing of land, geodesy.

*γεω-δαι-τικός: relating to geodesy, geodetic.

γεώδης (γεω+εἶδος): earth-like, earthy; geode.

*γεω-λόγ-ος: one who tells about the earth; hence *γεω-λογία, geology.

γεω-μέτρης: land-measurer, geometer.

γεω-μετρία: measurement of land, geometry.

γεω-μετρ-ικός: geometrical.

γεωργία: tillage of land, farming, agriculture.

γεωργικός: agricultural. georgic.

γεωργός (second part from root ἐργ): *one who works the ground, a farmer.*

γίγας, gen. γίγαντ-ος: *giant.*

γιγαντ-ικός: *like a giant, gigantic.*

γίγνομαι, syncopated from γι-γέν-ομαι (γεν): *become, come into being, be born.*

γι-γνώ-σκω (γνω): *know.*

γλῶσσα, γλῶττα: *tongue, speech, language.*

γνάθος: *the jaw.*

γνωσ-τικός (γιγνώσκω): *able to know,* gnostiϲ.

γράμμα, gen. γράμματ-ος: *what has been written, writing;* plur. γράμματα, *writings, documents, literature.*

γραμματ-ική < τέχνη >: *the art of writing,* grammar.

γραμματ-ικός: *pertaining to writing, skilled in writing,* grammatical.

γραφή: *drawing, painting, picture.*

γραφ-ικός: *like a picture,* graphic.

γράφω: *draw, paint, write.*

γυμνάζω (γυμναδ): from γυμνός: *exercise naked, exercise, train.*

γυμνάσιον: *a place for exercising or training,* a gymnasium.

γυμνασ-τής: *one who exercises, a trainer,* gymnast.

γυμνασ-τικός: *pertaining to exercising, or skilled in athletic exercises,* gymnastic.

γυμνός: *naked.*

γωνία: *a corner, angle.*

Δ

δαίμων: *a god or goddess, a divine being, a spirit;* in Christian writers, *an evil spirit,* demon. NOTE.—The word δαίμων is of much broader meaning than θεός and includes all sorts of supernatural beings. It may be used to designate the gods (οἱ θεοί), but more often is used of divine beings of lower rank than the gods. The term is often used of the spirit or genius which presides over a person's life for either good or evil. A person with a good genius was called εὐδαίμων, one with an evil genius δυσδαίμων, or κακοδαίμων.

δαίω: *divide.*

δάκρυ and δάκρυον: *a tear;* generally the plural is used for *tears,* but sometimes the sing. is used collectively in the sense of *tears.*

δακρύρροια (ῥέω): *a flowing of tears,* dacryrrhea.

δείκνυμι (δεικ): *show, point out.*

δένδρον: *tree.*

δέρμα, gen. δέρματος: *skin, hide.*

δεσπότης: *slave-master,* despot.

δεύτερος: *second.*

δέω: *bind, tie.*

δηλέ-ομαι: *hurt, harm.*

δηλη-τήριος: *harmful, noxious, poisonous,* deleterious.

δημ-αγωγικός: *like a demagogue,* demagogical.

δημ-αγωγός (δῆμος + ἄγω): *a leader of the people,* a demagogue, often in a bad sense.

δημο-κρατία: *rule by the people, popular government,* democracy.

δημο-κρατ-ικός: democratic, democrat.

δῆμος: the people, the common people.

δι-: a prefix meaning two.

διά: through, across; in compounds sometimes apart.

δια-βάλλω: throw apart, set at variance; especially by means of false accusations, hence slander, malign.

δια-βολικός: devilish, diabolical.

δια-βόλ-ος: slanderer, devil.

δια-γιγνώσκω: know things apart, distinguish, discern, decide.

διά-γνω-σις: a distinguishing and deciding, diagnosis.

διά-γωνος (γωνία): through the angles, diagonal.

διά-δημα (δέω): what is bound across or around one's head, diadem.

διά-θεσις: arrangement, disposition, condition, diathesis.

*διαθετικός: relating to the diathesis, diathetic.

διαίρεσις: separation, dieresis.

δι-αιρέω: take apart, separate.

δίαιτα: mode of life, kind of food, diet.

διαιτάω: feed in a certain way, diet.

διαιτη-τικός: relating to food, dietetic.

διάκονος: servant, minister, deacon.

δια-λέγομαι: talk back and forth, argue, converse.

δια-λεκ-τική < τέχνη>: the art of evolving truth by the method of question and answer, dialectic.

δια-λεκ-τικός: of the nature of conversation, skilled in argument, dialectical.

διά-λεκτος < γλῶσσα>: conversational language, dialect.

διά-λογος: conversation, dialogue.

διάμετρος < γραμμή>: the line measuring through or across, diameter.

δι-άρθρωσις: a joining apart, connection by a movable joint, diarthrosis.

διάρροια(ῥέω): a flowing through, diarrhea.

διά-στασις (ἵστημι): a standing apart, separation, diastasis.

διαστα-τικός: separative, relating to diastasis, diastatic.

διάστη-μα: interval.

δια-φαν-ής (φαίνω): showing through, transparent, diaphanous.

διά-φραγμα (φράσσω, stem φραγ): a wall through or across anything, a partition, diaphragm.

διδάσκω (διδαχ): teach.

δί-δω-μι (δο): give.

δί-λημμα (λαμβάνω): a double assumption, a double premiss, a dilemma. See λῆμμα.

διοίκεσις (δι-οικέω): housekeeping, administration, jurisdiction, diocese.

δίπλοος: two-fold, double.

διπλόω: double, fold.

δίπλω-μα: *a folded document, a letter of recommendation*, **diploma.**

διφθέρα: *a tanned hide, a piece of leather.*

δί-φθογγος: *having two sounds,* **a diphthong.**

δόγμα, gen. δόγματ-ος (δοκέω): *what seems best to one, opinion, conclusion;* in the case of those in authority *a decree, an ordinance,* **a dogma.**

δογματ-ικός: *of the nature of a decree or ordinance,* **dogmatic.**

δοκέω (δοκ), generally used in the third person singular as an impersonal verb, δοκεῖ: *it seems, it seems best.*

δόξα (δοκέω): *opinion, reputation, honor, glory.*

δοξο-λογία: *an expression of glory to God,* **doxology.**

δρᾶμα, gen. δράματ-ος (δράω): *what is done or acted out, deed, act,* **drama.**

δρασ-τικός: *active, effective,* **drastic.**

δραχμή: *drachme,* a weight, also a coin; Eng. **drachm.**

δράω: *do, perform.*

δρόμος: *a running, race, race-course, race-track.*

δρῦ-s: *a tree, an oak.*

δύνα-μαι: *be able, be powerful.*

δύνα-μις: *ability, power.*

δυνα-στεία: *lordship, domination,* **dynasty.**

δυνάστης: *lord, ruler, potentate.*

δυσ-: a prefix meaning *bad, badly, with difficulty.*

δῶρον: *gift.*

E

ἐγ-κέφαλος (ἐν+κεφαλή): *in the head;* as a noun, *brain;* neut. ἐγκέφαλον: **encephalon.**

ἐγώ: *I.*

ἐγ-χειρίδιον (χειρ): *a hand-book, manual,* **enchiridion.**

ἐθνικός: *relating to a nation, national,* **ethnic.**

ἔθνος: *a tribe, nation.*

εἶδος (stem εἰδες): *appearance, form, kind, species.*

εἰδύλλιον (diminutive of εἶδος): *a little image, a short, highly wrought descriptive poem on a pastoral subject, an* **idyl.**

εἴδωλον: *an image,* **idol.**

εἰδωλο-λατρεία: *idol-worship,* idolatry. Note that the English word drops out one syllable.

εἰκών: *image,* **icon.**

εἰρήνη: *peace;* hence the proper name, **Irene.**

εἰς: *into*

ἐκ, before a vowel, ἐξ: *out of.*

ἐκ-κεντρικός (κέντρον): *out of center,* **eccentric.**

ἐκ-λέγω: *pick out, select.*

ἐκ-λεκτικός: *inclined to select,* **eclectic.**

ἐκ-λογή: *a selection,* **eclogue.**

ἔκ-στα-σις (ἵστημι): *a standing outside of the proper place, a displacement, a being beside one's self*, ecstasy.

ἐκ-στα-τικός: *of the nature of ecstasy*, ecstatic.

ἐκ-τικός (ἔχω): *habitual, constitutional, consumptive*, hectic.

ἐκτομή (ἐκ-τέμνω): *a cutting out;* -ectomy in the latter part of medical terms.

ἐκτός: *outside, without.*

*ἐλασ-τικός, from ἐλαύνω (ἐλα) drive: *able to drive*, as a bent bow which drives the arrow by returning to its original form, elastic.

ἐλεγειακός: *having the nature of an elegy*, elegiac.

ἐλεγεῖον (ἔλεγος): *an elegiac couplet*, in the plural, *a poem made up of such couplets*, an elegy.

ἔλεγος: *a lament.*

ἐλεημοσύνη: *pity, mercy, charity,* alms.

ἔλεφας, gen. ἐλέφαντ-ος: elephant, *ivory.*

Ἕλλην: *a Greek*, a Hellene.

Ἑλληνίζω: *speak Greek, imitate the Greeks;* in active sense, *make a Greek of one,* Hellenize.

Ἑλλην-ικός: *Grecian*, Hellenic.

Ἑλληνισμός: *imitation of the Greeks, adoption of Greek language and civilization*, Hellenism.

Ἑλληνιστής: *one not of Greek race who uses the Greek language*, a Hellenist; in New Testament, *a Greek-Jew.*

*Ἑλληνιστικός: *relating to Hellenism and Hellenists*, Hellenistic.

ἐμ-βάλλω (βαλ, βλη): *throw in, put in, insert, inlay.*

ἔμ-βλημα: *something inserted or inlaid, an* emblem.

ἔμβρυον: *foetus*, embryo.

ἔμπλαστρον (πλάσσω): plaster, *salve.*

ἐμπόριον: *a trading place, port of entry,* emporium.

ἔμπορος (ἐν + πόρος): *a traveling merchant, importing merchant, wholesale merchant.*

ἔμφασις (ἐν + φαίνω): *a showing of something in or among other things so as to make it stand out prominently*, emphasis.

ἐμφατικός: *with emphasis*, emphatic.

ἐν: *in, among.*

ἔνδον: *inside, within.*

ἐνέργεια (ἐν + root ἐργ, work): *action*, energy.

ἐνεργέω: *be in action.*

ἐνεργη-τικός: *active*, energetic.

ἔν-θεος, contracted form, ἔνθους: *having the god in one's self, possessed by a god, inspired, frenzied.*

ἐνθουσιάζω: *be possessed by a god, be inspired.*

ἐνθουσιασμός: *inspiration*, en-thusiasm.

ἐνθουσιαστής: *one who is inspired*, enthusiast.

ἐνθουσιαστικός: *like an enthusiast*, enthusiastic.

ἔντερον: *entrail, intestine.*

ἔν-τομον (ἐν+τέμνω): *that which is cut into, insect.*

ἔξ-οδος: *a way out, a going out*, exodus.

ἔξω: *outside, without.*

ἐπ-εισ-όδιον (ὁδός, εἰσ-οδος, an entrance, a coming in): *something which comes in besides, or afterward, the part of a Greek tragedy between two choric songs, an* episode.

ἐπί: *upon, on, after, besides.*

ἐπί-γραμμα: *what is written upon a monument, an inscription in verse*, epigram.

ἐπι-γραφή: *an inscription.* This is the more general term for an inscription of any kind, hence epigraphy, the study of inscriptions.

ἐπί-θε-τον: *what is put upon, or added, an adjective*, epithet.

ἐπί-θη-μα: *something put on, a lid, cover, poultice*, epithem.

ἐπικός (ἔπος): epic.

ἐπι-λαμβάνω: *seize upon, lay hold of, attack.*

ἐπίληψις and ἐπιληψία: *a seizure, attack, fit*, epilepsy.

ἐπί-λογος: *after speech, concluding speech*, epilogue.

ἐπί-σκοπος (σκέπτομαι): *one who watches over, overseer, superintendent*, bishop. Hence the English word episcopal.

ἐπιστήμη: *knowledge, science;* sometimes contrasted with τέχνη, *art.*

ἐπι-στολή (ἐπι-στέλλω:) *a letter*, an epistle.

ἐπι-τίθημι: *put upon, add.*

ἐπι-τομή (ἐπι-τέμνω): *a cutting upon, an abridgement*, epitome, just as we say "a cutting down."

ἔπος, gen. ἔπε-ος (from root ἐπ, speak): *anything spoken,word, speech;* especially a line of heroic hexameter; in the plural, *heroic verses*, epic *poetry.*

ἐποχή (ἐπ-έχω): *a holding on, a waiting, the halting of a star a portion of time, an* epoch.

ἔργον: *work, deed, action.*

ἔρδω (ἐργ): *work, do.*

ἐρημία: *an uninhabited place, solitude, desert, wilderness.*

ἐρημί-της: *a man of the solitary place*, eremite, hermit.

ἐρυθρός: *red.*

ἔσω: *inside, within.*

ἑτερο-δοξία (δόξα): *wrong opinion or belief*, heterodoxy.

ἑτερό-δοξος: *having wrong opinion*, heterodox.

ἕτερος: *other of two, other than good or right, wrong.*

ἐτνμο-λογία: *telling the true sense of a word according to its origin, giving the etyma of words*, etymology.

ἔτυμον: *the true sense of a word according to its origin, the root-meaning, root of a word.*

ἔτυμος: *true, real.*

εὖ: *well, good.*

εὐαγγελίζομαι (εὐάγγελος): *bring good tidings, preach the gospel*, evangelize.

εὐαγγέλιον: *good news, glad tidings, the gospel.*

εὐάγγελος: *bringing good news; one who brings good news*, an evangel.

εὐγενής (γίγνομαι): *well born, noble.*

εὐλογία: *a speaking well of one, praise*, eulogy.

ἔχω (ἐχ, σεχ, ἐχ, σχε): *have, hold, hold oneself, keep oneself* <*so and so*>, *be* <*so and so*>.

Z

ζάω: *live, be alive.*

ζυγόν: *a yoke.*

ζωή: *life.*

ζώνη: *girdle, belt*, zone.

ζῷον: *a living being, animal.*

H

ἠθικός (ἦθος): *relating to moral character*, ethical; ἠθικά, ethics.

ἦθος: *character, moral character.*

ἤλεκτρον: *amber.*

ἥλιος: *the sun.*

ἡλιο-τρόπιον: heliotrope, so called because it turns to the sun.

ἡλιο-τρόπος (τρέπω): *turning to the sun.*

ἡμέρα: *day.*

ἡμι-: a prefix meaning *half.*

ἡμι-σφαίριον (σφαῖρα): a hemisphere.

ἧπαρ, gen. ἥπατ-ος: *liver.*

ἡπατ-ικός: *of the liver*, hepatic.

ἥρως: *warrior*, hero.

ἠχώ: echo.

Θ

θάλαμος: *inner room, bed-chamber.*

θεά-ομαι: *see, observe, gaze upon.*

θέα-τρον: *a place for seeing, a* theater.

θέ-μα (τίθημι): *what is put down for discussion, a proposition*, theme.

θεο-λογ-ία: *a telling about the gods, or about God*, theology.

θεο-λογ-ικός: theological.

θεο-λόγ-ος: *one who tells about the gods, or God, a* theologian.

θεός: *a god, God.*

θεραπεία: *service, attendance, care of the sick, treatment of disease*, therapy.

θεραπευ-τικός: *relating to care of the sick, or to medical treatment*, therapeutic.

θεραπεύω: *serve, care for, give medical treatment to.*

θερμός: *warm, hot.*

VOCABULARY

θεωρέω: *view, contemplate, speculate, philosophize.*

θεώρη-μα: *that which is viewed or contemplated;* in mathematics, *a theorem.*

θεωρη-τικός: *contemplative, speculative, theoretical.*

θεωρία: *a view, a theory.*

θεωρός: *a spectator, sight-seer, delegate to a religious festival, or to the national games.*

θρίξ, gen. τριχ-ός: *hair.*

θώραξ: *breast-plate, part of the body covered by the breast-plate, chest,* thorax.

I

ιάομαι: *heal, cure.*

ιατρεία: *healing, medical treatment.*

ιατρικός: *relating to a physician, or to medical treatment, curative, medical.*

ιατρός: *a physician,* or *surgeon.*

Ἴδα: *a wooded hill,* Mount Ida.

ιδέα (from root ἰδ, *see, appear*): *appearance, form, image, mental image,* idea.

ἴδιος: *one's own, private, personal, peculiar.*

ιδιο-συγκρασία (συγκεράννυμι): *one's own mixture, peculiar temperament or habit,* idiosyncrasy.

ιδίωμα, gen. ιδιώματ-ος: *a peculiarity,* especially *a peculiarity of speech,* idiom.

ιδιώτης: *a private person; one who is unskilled, ignorant, or stupid.* Eng. deriv., idiot.

ιερ-άρχης (ἄρχω): *a ruler of sacred things, high priest,* hierarch.

ιερ-αρχία: *rule of a hierarch,* hierarchy.

ιερός: *sacred.*

ἵππος: *a horse.*

ἴρις: *rainbow, halo,* a flower, *the* iris; *the iris of the eye;* name of a goddess, Iris.

ἴσος: *equal.*

ἵστημι (στα): *stand, set up.*

ιστορία: *inquiry, research, knowledge gained by inquiry or research, a written report of such knowledge, narrative,* history, *story.*

ιστός: *loom, web.*

ιχθύς: *fish.*

K

καθαίρω (καθαρ): *cleanse, purify, purge.*

καθαρός: *clean, pure.*

καθαρ-τικός: *cleansing, purgative,* cathartic.

καθέδρα: *seat, chair, bishop's chair;* hence cathedral.

καθολικός (κατά+ὅλος): *relating to the whole, general, universal,* catholic.

καίω (καυ): *burn.*

καλλι-: form which the stem of καλός, *beautiful,* usually takes at the beginning of a compound.

καλός: *beautiful, noble, good.*

κάλυξ, gen. κάλυκ-ος: *seed-pod, cup of a flower,* calyx.

κανών: *straight rod, straight-edge, rule,* canon.

καρδία: *heart.*

καρδια-κός: *pertaining to the heart,* cardiac.

καρκίνος: *a crab; a cancer.*

καρπός: *fruit, grain, produce.*

καρπός: *the wrist,* carpus.

κατά: *down; in accordance with.*

κατα-βάλλω: *throw down, over-throw, destroy.*

κατα-βολή: *a throwing down.*

*κατα-βολικός: *tending to throw down, destructive,* catabolic.

*κατα-βολισμός: *a throwing down,* catabolism.

κατα-λέγω: *pick out, enlist, enrol.*

κατά-ληψις (κατα-λαμβάνω): *a seizing,* catalepsy.

κατά-λογος (κατα-λέγω): *a register, a roll, list,* catalog.

κατά-λυσις (κατα-λύω): *a loosing, a dissolving,* catalysis.

κατα-λύω: *dissolve, break up.*

κατ-αράσσω (ἀραγ): *dash down;* κατ-αράκ-της: *down-dasher,* cataract.

κατα-ρ-ρέω (ῥέω): *flow down.*

κατάρροος: *flowing down;* as a noun, *a running from the head or nose,* catarrh.

κατα-στρέφω: *turn down, upset, overthrow.*

κατα-στροφή: *an overturning, sudden reverse,* catastrophe.

κατ-ηγορία: *an accusation, declaration, predicate,* category.

καυσ-τικός (καίω, root καυ, *burn*): *inclined to burn,* caustic.

καυ-τήρ (καίω): *a burner, a branding iron.*

καυτηριάζω: *sear,* cauterize.

καυ-τήριον: *a branding iron;* also *a brand,* cautery.

κενός: *empty.*

κέντρον: *a sharp point, a goad, a puncture, the puncture made by the stationary limb of the compass in drawing a circle, the center of a circle,* center.

κεράννυμι (κερα, κρα): *mix.*

κέρας, gen. κέρατ-ος: *a horn.*

κεφαλή: *head.*

κλάδος: *a young shoot, a twig, a branch.*

κλάω: *break.*

κλέπ-της: *a thief.*

κλέπτω (κλεπ): *steal.*

κλῖμαξ, gen. κλίμακ-ος: *a ladder, a stair-case,* climax.

κλίνη: *couch, bed.*

κλινικός: *pertaining to a bed, or beds; a physician who visits the sick in their beds,* clinical.

κόγχη: *a shell-fish, a shell.*

κοῖλος: *hollow.*

κοιλόω: *make hollow, hollow out.*

κοίλω-μα, gen. κοιλώματ-ος: *a hollow, a cavity.*

κοιμάω: *put to sleep;* κοιμάομαι: *go to sleep.*

κοιμη-τήριον: *sleeping place,* cemetery.

κολεός: *a sheath, a scabbard;* in Aristotle, *the sheath or shard of a beetle's wings.*

κόμη: *the hair of the head,* especially of *long hair.*

κομή-της: *a long-haired fellow; a comet.*

κόμμα (κόπτω, strike, cut): *what is cut off, a short clause.* In English the point used to mark off a short clause, *a* comma.

κόρη, κόρα: *a girl, a maiden.*

Κορίνθιος: Corinthian.

Κόρινθος: Corinth.

κοσμέω: *order, arrange, adon.*

κοσμη-τικός: *suited for adorning,* cosmetic.

κοσμο-γονία (κόσμος and γίγνομαι): *birth or origin of the universe,* cosmogony.

κοσμο-πολίτης: *a citizen of the world,* cosmopolite.

κόσμος: *order, adornment; the universe, the world.*

κοτύλη: *a cup.*

κοτυληδών: *anything cup-shaped.* In botany *a* cotyledon.

κρά-σις (κεράννυμι): *a mixing, blending, combination,* crasis.

κρα-τήρ: *a mixer, mixing-bowl, bowl,* crater.

κράτος: *strength, power, rule.*

κρίνω (κρι): *separate, distinguish, decide, judge.*

κρί-σις: *a decision, judgment, decisive point,* crisis.

κρι-τήριον: *a means of judging, a* criterion.

κρι-τής: *a judge.*

κρι-τικός: *able to judge, critical;* as noun, *a* critic.

κρόκος: *saffron.* Hence Eng. crocus.

κρυπ-τός: *hidden, concealed;* κρυπτόν: *a* crypt.

κρύπτω (κρυφ): *hide, conceal.*

κρύσταλλος: *ice; rock-crystal,* crystal.

κτείς, gen. κτεν-ός: *a comb, a rake, a cockle.*

κύβος: *a cube, a die* for playing dice.

κυκλάμινος (κύκλος): cyclamen.

κύκλος: *a circle,* cycle.

κύλινδρος: *a roller, a* cylinder.

κυλίνδω: *roll.*

κυνός-ουρα: *a dog's tail,* name of a constellation, cynosure.

Κῦρος: Cyrus.

κύστις: *a bladder, a pouch;* cyst.

κύτος: *a hollow, a hollow thing, a vase, a jar.* In modern science, *a cell,* cyte.

κύων, gen. κυν-ός: *a dog.*

κῶλον: *a limb, a member; a member of a sentence, a* colon.

κωμικός: *of the nature of a revel, or of a comedy,* comic.

κῶμος: *a revel, a band of revellers, the ode sung by a band of revellers, a* comus.

κωμ-ῳδία (ἀείδω, sing. ἀοιδός, singer): revel-song, comedy.

κῶνος: a cone.

Λ

Λάκων: a Laconian, or Lacedaemonian, a Spartan.

Λακωνικός: Laconian, like a Laconian, laconic.

λαμβάνω (λαβ, ληβ): take, take hold of, seize.

λαός: people, men.

λάρυγξ, gen. λάρυγγ-ος: upper part of the windpipe, larynx; also used loosely for throat.

λατρεία: service.

λέγω: say, speak, tell.

λέγω: pick, gather, count, reckon.

λειτουργία (from λέϊτος, of the people, public, and root ἐργ, work); a working for the people, public service, liturgy.

λεξικός, -όν (λέξις): relating to words, or speech; λεξικόν < βιβλίον > : a word book, dictionary, lexicon.

λέξις (λέγω): speech, word.

λευκός: white.

λέων, gen. λέοντ-ος: lion; proper name Leon.

ληθαργία: drowsiness, lethargy.

λήθαργος (λήθη): forgetful, drowsy, lethargic.

λήθη: forgetfulness, lethe.

λῆμμα (λαμβάνω): what is taken, or assumed, an assumption, a premiss, lemma. Cf. δί-λημμα.

λίθος: stone.

λογικός (λόγος): reasonable, logical; λογική < τέχνη > : the art of reasoning, logic.

λογο-γράφος: a speech-writer, logographer.

λόγος (λέγω): word, speech, reason, account.

λύρα: a lyre.

λυρικός: relating to the lyre, lyric, lyrical.

λύω: loose, loosen, dissolve.

M

μαγικός (Μάγος): belonging to or suited to a Magian, or magician; magic, magical.

Μαγνῆτις < λίθος > : the Magnesian stone, magnet.

Μάγος: a Magian, a Persian priest and wise man; a wizard, a magician.

μάθημα (μανθάνω): what is learnt, a lesson, learning, knowledge, especially mathematical knowledge.

μαθηματ-ικός: fond of learning, concerned with learning, mathematical; τὰ μαθηματικά, mathematics.

μαίνομαι (μαν): rage, rave, be mad, be crazy, be inspired.

μαλακός: soft.

μανθάνω (μαθ, μαθε): learn, understand.

μαν-ία (μαίνομαι): madness, frenzy, insanity, mania.

μάν-τις: an inspired person, a seer, a prophet.

μαργαρίτης: *a pearl.*

μάρτυς, μάρτυρ-ος: *a witness;* in ecclesiastical language, a martyr.

Μαυσωλεῖον: *tomb of Mausolus,* mausoleum.

Μαύσωλος: *Mausolus king of Halicarnassus.*

μέγας (stems μεγα and μεγαλο): *large, big, great.*

Μέδουσα: Medusa, a Gorgon with snaky locks the sight of whom turned people to stone.

μέθοδος (μετά and ὁδός): *a going after, pursuit of knowledge, process,* method.

μεθύω: *be drunken.*

μέλας, μέλαν-ος: *black.*

μέλισσα: *a bee;* hence proper name Melissa.

μέλος: *song, tune, music.*

μελῳδία (μέλος+ᾄδω): *tune-singing,* melody.

μεσ-εντέριον < δέρμα> (μέσος+ ἔντερον): mesentery.

μέσος: *in the middle, between, middle, mid.*

μετά: *with, among, after;* in composition often denoting change like the Latin *trans, across* (trans), *differently.*

μετα-βάλλω: *place differently, change, transpose.*

μεταβολή: *a changing, change, transition.*

μεταβολικός: *relating to change, changeable;* metabolic.

*μεταβολισμός: metabolism.

μετά-θεσις (τίθημι): *a placing across, transposition,* metathesis.

μέταλλον: *a mine;* in late Greek, a metal.

*μεταλλουργία (ἔργ): *mine-working, metal-working,* metallurgy.

μεταλλουργός: *one who works mines, or metals, a miner;* metallurgist.

*μετα-μορφικός (μορφή): of *changed form,* metamorphic.

*μετά-μορφος: *with changed form,* metamorphous.

μετα-μορφόω: *change the form of, transform,* metamorphose.

μετα-μόρφωσις: *transformation,* metamorphosis.

μετα-φέρω: *carry across, transfer.*

μετα-φορά: *transference,* especially of a word to a new sense, metaphor.

μετέωρος: *lifted up, on high, in the heavens;* μετέωρον, *a heavenly body,* meteor.

μέτρον: *measure.*

μήτηρ, gen. μητρ-ός: *mother.*

μητρόπολις: *mother city, chief city,* metropolis.

μηχανή: *a contrivance, a machine.*

μιαίνω (μιαν): *defile, pollute.*

μίασ-μα: *pollution,* miasma.

μικρός: *small, little*

μιμέομαι: *imitate.*

μίμη-σις: *imitation,* mimesis.

μιμη-τικός: *imitative,* mimetic.

μιμικός (μῖμος): *like an imitator,* mimic.

μῖμος: *an imitator, an impersonator;* also a mime, a little dramatic composition depicting scenes from every-day life.

μισ-άνθρωπος: *hating mankind,* misanthropic.

μισέω: *hate.*

μισο-γύνης: *hating women; a woman-hater,* a misogynist.

μισογυνία: *hatred of women,* misogyny.

μῖσος: *hate, hatred.*

μοναχός (μόνος): *solitary; a solitary man,* monk.

μονο-πωλία (πωλέω, sell): *a lone-selling, exclusive sale,* monopoly.

μόνος: *alone, only;* in compounds, *single, one.*

μονό-τονος: *of a single tone,* monotonous.

Μορφεύς (μορφή): *the former, maker of the forms and images seen in sleep, the god of dreams,* Morpheus; hence morphine, morphia.

μορφή: *form, shape.*

μορφόω: *give form to, form, shape.*

μόρφωσις: *a forming, shaping,* morphosis.

Μοῦσα: *goddess of song and inspiration,* Muse.

Μουσ-εῖον: *temple of the Muses, a school of art and poetry, a library,* museum.

μουσ-ικὴ < τέχνη > : *the art of the Muses,* music.

μουσ-ικός: *of or for the Muses,* musical.

μύελος: *marrow, spinal cord, brain.*

μυέω (μύω): *initiate into the mysteries.*

μυθο-λογέω: *tell myths or legends.*

μυθο-λογία: *the telling of myths or legends,* mythology.

μυθο-λόγος (λέγω): *a teller of legends,* mythologist.

μῦθος: *a speech, tale, story, legend,* myth.

μύκης, gen. μύκητ-ος: *a mushroom, fungus.*

μυστήριον (μυέω, μύω): *a secret doctrine,* mystery.

μύστης: *one who has been initiated into the mysteries.*

μυστικός: *secret,* mystic.

μύω: *close the eyes, close the mouth.*

N

Ναϊάς, gen. Ναϊάδ-ος (νάω): *a river-nymph, a fountain-nymph,* Naiad.

νάρκη: *numbness.*

νάρκισσος: narcissus, name of a plant and its flower.

ναρκόω (νάρκη): *benumb.*

νάρκω-σις: *a benumbing,* narcosis.

ναρκω-τικός: *able to benumb, benumbing,* narcotic.

ναῦς: *a ship.*

ναυσία, also written ναυτία: *ship sickness, sea-sickness,* nausea.

ναύ-της: *ship-man, seaman,* sailor.

ναυτ-ικός: *relating to sailors,* nautical.

νάω: *flow.*

νεκρο-μαντεία (μάντις): *prophecy by means of the dead,* that is, by calling up their spirits, necromancy.

νεκρός: *a dead body, a corpse;* also as an adjective, *dead;* in plural, οἱ νεκροί, *the dead.*

νεκρόω: *make dead, mortify.*

νέκρω-σις: *a deadening, deadness,* necrosis.

νέκταρ: *the drink of the gods,* nectar.

νέμεσις (νέμω): *a dealing out of what is due, righteous indignation, divine wrath, divine retribution,* nemesis; personified as *the goddess of retribution,* Nemesis.

νέμω (νεμ, νεμε): *deal out, distribute, arrange, manage; feed, pasture.*

νέος: *new, young.*

νεῦρον: *sinew, tendon, cord;* in late writers, especially the physician Galen, *a nerve.*

νεφρῖτις: *kidney disease, inflammation of the kidneys,* nephritis.

νεφρός: *the kidneys, a kidney.*

νίκη: *victory.*

νομαδ-ικός: *like the nomads,* nomadic.

νομάς, gen. νομάδ-ος (νέμω): *a herdsman,* nomad.

νόμος (νέμω): *what is dealt out or established by custom or legislation, custom, convention,* law.

νομός (νέμω): *a pasture, a district, a* nome.

νόσος: *disease, sickness.*

νύμφη: *a bride, a young woman, a* nymph.

νῶτον: *the back.*

Ξ

ξιφο-ειδής (εἶδος): *having the form or appearance of a sword* (ξίφος), *sword-shaped,* xiphoid.

ξίφος: *sword.*

O

ὁ, ἡ, τό: definite article in its three genders, *the.*

ὁδός: *road, way, journey, a going.*

ὀδύνη: *pain.*

οἰκέω: *dwell, live in, inhabit.*

οἰκο-νομία (οἶκος and νέμω): *management of a house, estate, or property; good management, thrift,* economy.

οἰκο-νομικός: *skilled in financial management, thrifty,* economical.

οἰκο-νόμος: *manager of a house, or an estate, manager, administrator, business manager.*

οἶκος: *house, home, estate, property.*

οἴσω, future of verb φέρω: *bear, carry.*

ὀλίγος: *little, few.*

ὅλος: *whole, entire, all.*

'Ολύμπιος: *Olympian.*

"Ολυμπος: *Olympus, Mount Olympus, home of the gods.*

ὁμαλός: *even, level.*

ὁμο-γενής (ὁμος+γένος): *of the same race, of the same kind,* homogeneous.

ὁμοῖος: *of the same sort, like.*

ὁμοιο-πάθεια: *a being affected in like manner, likeness of suffering.* Hence homeopathy.

ὁμός: *same.*

ὄνομα, gen. ὀνόματ-ος; old form generally used in second part of a compound, ὄνυμα: *name.* Compare ἀν-ώνυμος, anonymous.

ὀξύς: *sharp, keen, acid;* of sounds, *sharp, shrill;* of motion, *swift.*

ὀπ, root found in some tenses of ὀράω: *see.*

ὀπ-τικός: *pertaining to seeing or sight,* optical; ὀπτικά, *things belonging to vision,* optics.

ὀράω (ὀρα, ὀπ, ιδ; an irregular verb showing three entirely different stems in its different tenses): *see.*

ὄργανον (from root ἐργ, *work*): *a tool, an instrument, an* organ.

ὀρθό-δοξος (ὀρθός+δόξα): *of right opinion,* orthodox.

ὀρθός: *straight, upright, right.*

ὀρίζω (ὅρος): *bound, limit.*

ὀρίζων <κύκλος>: *the bounding circle,* horizon.

ὄρνις, gen. ὄρνιθ-ος: *bird, fowl.*

ὅρος: *boundary, border, limit, definition.*

ὀρφανός: *without parents, fatherless,* orphan.

ὀρχέομαι: *dance.*

ὀρχηστικός: *suited for dancing, relating to dancing,* orchestic.

ὀρχήστρα: *a dancing place, the* orchestra or *dancing place in a Greek theater.*

ὀστέον: *a bone.*

ὀστρακίζω (ὄστρακον): *to banish by votes written on potsherds,* ostracize.

ὀστρακισμός: ostracism.

ὄστρακον: *a potsherd, a clay tablet used in voting; a shell.*

οὐρά: *tail.*

οὖρον: *urine.*

οὖς, gen. ὠτ-ός: *ear.*

ὀφθαλμός: *eye.*

ὄχλος: *a crowd, a mob.*

Π

παθητικός: *able to feel, sensitive; suited to arouse feeling,* pathetic.

*παθο-λογία: *the science of diseases,* pathology.

παθο-λογικός: *relating to telling about diseases, concerned with the science of diseases,* pathological, παθολογική <τέχνη> was the ancient Greek term for *pathology.*

VOCABULARY 83

πάθος (πάσχω): feeling, suffering, disease.
παιδ-αγωγία: the office of a παιδαγωγός. Eng. deriv. pedagogy.
παιδ-αγωγός (παῖς+ἄγω): a boyleader, a trusty slave who cared for a boy, took him to school, and brought him home after school was over. The school teacher was called διδάσκαλος. The English word pedagogue, derived from παιδαγωγός, has the meaning of the Greek word διδάσκαλος.
παιδευ-τικός: of or for teaching, instructional, paedeutic.
παιδεύω (παῖς): bring up a child, train, teach.
παῖς, gen. παιδ-ός: child, boy, girl.
Παιών, also Παιάν: Apollo as god of healing, Paeon; a song of thanksgiving, or triumph, originally addressed to Apollo as Paeon or god of healing, a paean.
παιώνιος: belonging to Paeon, healing, medicinal; hence παιωνία, peony, supposed to be medicinal in ancient times.
παν-άκεια: a cure-all, panacea.
παν-ακής (ἀκέομαι): all-healing.
*παν-όραμα (ὁράω): a seeing of all, panorama.
παντό-μιμος: an imitator of all, an actor in a dumb-show. Hence Eng. pantomime.
παρά: beside, by the side of; also beside in the sense of in violation of, contrary to.

παρα-βάλλω: throw beside, place beside, compare.
παρα-βολή: a placing beside, a comparison, a parable; also in mathematics a parabola.
παράδεισος: a park, paradise.
παρά-δοξος: beside or contrary to opinion, incredible, paradoxical; παράδοξον, a paradox.
παρ-άλληλος (ἀλλήλοιν): beside one another, side by side, parallel.
παρά-σιτος (σῖτος, food): one who eats at another's table, a parasite.
παρά-φρασις: a telling beside, a retelling in different form, a paraphrase.
παρ-έν-θεσις: a putting in beside, an insertion, a parenthesis.
παρενθετικός: parenthetic.
πᾶς, gen. παντ-ός, neut. nom. πᾶν: all, every.
πάσχω (παθ, παθε): be acted upon, be affected, suffer, feel, experience.
πατήρ, gen. πατρ-ός: father.
πατριά: a group of people descended from a common father, a clan, a tribe, a family, a race.
πατριάρχης: a ruler of a tribe, or race, chief of the tribe, father of the race, patriarch. In ecclesiastical usage the bishop of an important city or district, as the patriarch of Rome, of Antioch, etc.

πατριαρχία: *the office of a patri-arch,* a patriarchy.

πατριώτης (πατριᾱ): *a clans-man, tribesman, countryman, citizen;* especially one who was loyal to his clan, tribe, or country, a patriot.

παχύ-δερμος: *thick-skinned, pach-ydermous;* παχύδερμον<ζῶον>, a pachyderm.

παχύς: *thick.*

πεῖρα: *trial, attempt, attack.*

πειρατής: *one who attacks,* a pirate.

πειράω: *try, attempt, attack.*

πέμπω: *send, escort.*

πεντά-γωνος (γωνία): *having five angles,* pentagonal, pentagon.

πέντε: *five,* usually πεντα- at the beginning of a compound word.

περί: *around, about.*

περί-μετρον: *measure around, circumference,* perimeter.

περί-οδος: *a going around, a circuit, a cycle of time, a period; a well-rounded sen-tence,* a period.

περί-στυλον (στῦλος): *a row of columns around a building or court, a colonnade,* a peristyle.

περι-τόναιον (τείνω): *that which is stretched around, the* peri-tonaeum.

περί-φρασις: *a talking around, circumlocution,* periphrasis.

πέσσω (πεπ): *soften, cook, digest.*

-ἰταλον: *leaf,* petal.

πέψις (πέσσω): *cooking, diges-tion.*

πίπτω (πετ, πτω): *fall.*

πλάνης, gen. πλάνητ-ος: *a wan-derer, a wandering star,* a planet.

πλάσ-μα (πλάσσω): *what is formed or molded, a formation;* plasm in protoplasm, etc.

πλάσσω (πλατ): *form, mold, shape.*

πλασ-τικός: *capable of being molded, relating to molding,* plastic.

πλευρά: *a rib, the ribs, the side* of a human being or animal.

πληγή: *a stroke, a blow, a* plague.

πληθώρη: *fullness,* plethora.

πληθωρικός: plethoric.

πλοῦτος: *riches, wealth.*

πνεῦμα (πνέω): *wind, air, breath, spirit.*

πνευματ-ικός: *having to do with wind or air,* pneumatic.

πνεύμων: *the lungs.*

πνέω (πνευ): *breathe, blow.*

ποιέω: *make, compose.*

ποίημα: *what is made, a work, composition,* poem.

ποίησις: *creation, poetry,* poesy.

ποιητής: *maker, composer,* poet.

πολεμικός: *warlike,* polemic.

πόλεμος: *war.*

πολιός: *gray.*

πόλις: *city, state.*

πολίτης: *citizen.*

πολυ-γαμία: *a being much married, or having many wives,* polygamy.

πολύ-γαμος (γαμέω): *often married,* polygamous.

πολύ-γωνος (γωνία): *having many angles,* polygonal.

πολύ-μορφος: *having many forms,* polymorphous.

πολύς: *much, many.*

πομπή (πέμπω): *a sending, an escort, parade, procession,* pomp.

πόρος: *way, passage,* pore.

ποταμός: *river.*

πούς, gen. ποδ-ός: *foot.*

πρᾶγμα, gen. πράγματ-ος (πράσσω): *that which has been done, deed, act, fact, thing, matter, affair, business.*

πραγματικός: *suited for affairs or business, business-like, practical, having to do with matter of fact,* pragmatic, pragmatical.

πρακτικός: *fit for action, able to accomplish, effective,* practical.

πρᾶξις: *a doing, transaction, accomplishing.*

πράσσω (πρᾱγ): *do, accomplish.*

πρεσβύτερος: *elder; an elder,* presbyter.

πρίσμα: *that which has been sawn,* prism.

πρίω: *saw,* i.e., cut with a saw.

πρό: *before, for, forth.*

προ-βάλλω (βαλ, βλη): *throw before, place before, put forward, propose.*

πρό-βλημα: *what is put forward, or proposed, proposition,* problem.

προ-βληματικός: *like a problem,* problematic.

πρό-λογος: *a speech before, a fore-word,* prologue.

προ-παιδεία: *preparatory teaching.*

*προ-παιδευτικός: *suited for preparatory instruction,* propaedeutic. See παιδεύω.

πρωτ-αγωνιστής: *first contestant, chief contestant,* protagonist.

πρῶτος: *first.*

προ-φήτης (φημί): *one who speaks for a god and interprets his will, an interpreter,* prophet; also *one who speaks forth, or proclaims;* later, *one who foretells, or predicts.*

προ-φυλακτικός (φυλάσσω): *able to guard before, preventive,* prophylactic.

πτέρον: *wing.*

πτῶμα (πίπτω): *a fallen body, corpse, carcass.*

πύον: *discharge from a sore,* pus.

πυόω: *suppurate.*

πῦρ: *fire.*

πυραμίς, gen. πυραμίδ-ος: a pyramid.

πυρή: *a funeral fire,* pyre.

πυρόω: *burn, set on fire, inflame.*

πύρωσις: *a burning,* pyrosis.

πύωσις (πυόω): *suppuration,* pyosis.

πωλέω: *sell.*

P

ῥεῦμα: *a flow, current, stream;* med. *a discharge,* rheum.

ῥέω (ῥε, ῥευ, ῥυ): *flow.*

ῥήγνυμι (ῥηγ, ῥαγ): *break.* Compare hemorrhage.

ῥή-τωρ (from root ῥε, *speak*): *a speaker, orator,* rhetor. Hence ῥητορ-ικός, rhetorical, and ῥητορική <τέχνη>, *the art of speaking,* rhetoric.

ῥινοκέρως (ῥίς+κέρας, *horn*): *nose-horn,* rhinoceros.

ῥίς, gen. ῥιν-ός: *nose.*

ῥόδον: *a rose.*

ῥυθμός (ῥέω): *flow,* rhythm.

Σ

σαρκάζω (σαρκαδ): *tear the flesh, bite the lips in rage, speak biting words.*

σαρκασμός: *mockery,* sarcasm.

*σαρκαστικός: sarcastic.

σαρκο-φάγος: *flesh-eating, flesh-eater,* sarcophagus.

σάρξ, gen. σαρκ-ός: *flesh.*

σάτυρος: *a* satyr. The satyrs were imaginary creatures, half man and half goat, which formed the retinue of Dionysus the god of wine, who was also called Bacchus.

σεισμός: *a shaking, an earthquake.*

σείω: *shake, quake.*

σῆμα: *a sign.*

σηπ-τικός: *productive of decay,* septic.

σήπω: *make rotten; rot, decay.*

σῆψις: *a rotting, decay, putrefaction,* sepsis.

σθένος (σθενες): *strength.*

σῖτος: *grain, bread, food.*

σκάνδαλον: *a trap, snare;* scandal.

σκελετόν: *a dried-up body, mummy,* skeleton.

σκέλλω: *make dry, dry up.*

σκεπ-τικός: *inclined to look at and examine,* skeptical.

σκέπτομαι (σκεπ): *look, look at, examine, consider.*

σκηνή: *a tent, a booth; the tent or building which formed the background in a Greek theater,* scene.

σκῆπ-τρον: *staff,* scepter.

σκήπτω (σκηπ): *prop, prop one's self, lean upon.*

σκληρός: *hard, stiff.*

*σκληρόω: harden.

σκλήρωσις: *a hardening,* sclerosis.

*σκληρωτικός: *hard, stiff,* sclerotic.

σκοπός (σκέπτομαι): *a looker, look-out, watcher; the object at which one looks, mark, aim,* scope.

σοφία: *wisdom.*

σοφίζω, mid. σοφίζομαι: *be wise, act wise, be crafty, pretend to be wise.*

σόφισμα: *a sly trick, quibble, fallacy,* sophism.

σοφιστής: *a wise man, a professor of wisdom, a pretender to wisdom,* **sophist.**

σοφός: *wise.*

σπασμός (σπάω): *a convulsion,* **spasm.**

σπασμώδης (εἶδος): *like a spasm,* **spasmodic.**

σπάω: *draw, pull, wrench, convulse.*

σπείρω (σπερ): *scatter, sow.*

σπέρμα, gen. σπέρματ-ος: *what is sown, seed.*

σπλήν: *the* **spleen.**

σπορά (σπείρω): *sowing, seed.*

σπόρος: *sowing, seed,* **spore.**

στά-σις (ἵστημι): *a standing, state, condition.*

στα-τικός: *causing to stand still, standing still,* **static.**

στέλλω (στελ): *send, despatch.*

στερεός: *solid.*

στέρνον: *the breast, chest;* in modern medicine, *breastbone,* **sternum.**

στέφανος: *a wreath, garland, crown.*

στίγμα: *a prick made with a pointed instrument, puncture, mark, brand,* **stigma.**

στόμαχος: *throat, gullet;* late Greek, **stomach.**

στρατηγέω: *be a general, exercise generalship.*

στρατήγημα: *an act of generalship, a* **stratagem.**

στρατηγία: *generalship,* **strategy.**

στρατηγικός: *suited for a general,* **strategic.**

στρατηγός (στρατός+ἄγω): *an army-leader, general.*

στρατός: *army, camp.*

στρέφω: *turn.*

στροφή: *a turning;* a portion of a song sung during a turn or evolution of the chorus, a **strophe,** *a* **stanza.**

στῦλος: *pillar, post, column.*

συγ-χόνδρωσις (χόνδρος): *a uniting of cartilage, or by means of cartilage.* **synchondrosis.**

συλάω: *strip off, carry off, plunder.*

συλ-λαβή: *what is taken together, a* **syllable.**

συλ-λαμβάνω (λαβ, ληβ): *take together.*

συλ-λέγω: *gather, collect.*

συλ-λογή: *a gathering together, a collection,* **sylloge.**

συλλογίζομαι: *collect or conclude from premises, reason, infer, conclude.*

συλλογισμός: *a conclusion from premises, an argument from premises, a* **syllogism.**

σύμβολον (βάλλω): *what is put together with something, a sign or token by which something, or some person, is recognized, a token, sign, badge,* **symbol.**

συμ-πάθεια: *a feeling with one, a fellow-feeling,* **sympathy.**

συμ-παθέω: *feel with one,* **sympathize.**

88   EVERYDAY GREEK

συμπαθητικός: *able to feel with one*, sympathetic.

συμ-πίπτω (πτω): *fall together with, happen with, occur with.*

σύμπτωμα: *what occurs with anything, a symptom.*

σύμφυσις (φύω): *a growing together*, symphysis.

συμφωνία (φωνή): *a sounding with, a concord of sounds*, symphony.

σύμφωνος: *sounding together, accordant, harmonious.*

σύν: *with, together with, together.*

σύν in compounds takes different forms, depending upon the letter which follows it, and so appears as συν-, συλ-, συμ-, συ-.

συν-αγωγή (ἄγω): *a bringing together, an assembly, a meeting, a place of meeting*, synagogue.

συν-άρθρωσις: *a joining together, union by an immovable joint*, synarthrosis. See ἄρθρωσις.

σύν-δεσμος (δέω): *that which binds together, a band, bond; a binding together, like* σύνδεσις.

*συν-δέσμωσις: *a binding together*, syndesmosis.

σύν-θε-σις (τίθημι): *a putting together*, synthesis.

συν-θε-τικός (τίθημι): *able to put together, constructive*, synthetic.

συν-ίστημι: *set together, stand together.*

σύν-οδος (ὁδός): *a coming together, meeting*, synod.

συν-τακτικός (τάσσω): *relating to arranging together, having to do with syntax*, syntactical.

σύν-ταξις: *an arranging together, primarily of soldiers in an army; in grammar*, syntax.

συν-τίθημι: *put together, construct.*

σῦριγξ, gen. σύριγγ-ος: *a shepherd's pipe, Panspipe*, syrinx; *a pipe*, or *tube*. Eng. syringe.

σύ-στημα (συν-ίστημι): *anything set together, an organized whole*, system.

συστηματικός: systematic.

σφαῖρα: *a ball, globe*, sphere.

σφαιρο-ειδής (εἶδος): *like a sphere*, spheroid.

σφίγγω: *bind, tie.*

σφιγκτήρ: *a binder, band*, sphincter.

Σφίγξ, gen. σφιγγ-ός: *the* Sphinx.

σφυγμο-ειδής: *like a pulse*, sphygmoid.

σφυγμός: *a throbbing, the beating of the heart, the pulse.*

σφύζω (σφυγ): *throb, beat, pulsate.*

σχῆμα, gen. σχήματ-ος (ἔχω): *the way a thing holds itself, form, figure, appearance, bearing, character, plan*, scheme.

σχίζω (σχιδ): *split, cleave.*

σχίσμα: *a cleft, split, division*, schism.

σχισματ-ικός: *like a schism*, schismatic.

*σχιστο-γλωσσία: *a congenital fissure or cleft of the tongue.*

*σχιστό-κυτος: *a split cell,* schistocyte.

σχιστός: *split, cleft, divided, divisible;* schist.

σχολάζω (σχολαδ): *have leisure, attend lectures of a philosopher, devote one's self to learning.*

σχολαστικός: *inclined to learning; a scholar,* scholastic.

σχολή: *leisure; leisure spent in learning, learned discussion, lecture; the place of lectures and discussions,* school.

T

τακ-τικός (τάσσω): *able to arrange or draw up troops, relating to the arrangement of soldiers,* tactical; τακτικά: *matters relating to the arrangement of troops,* tactics.

τάξις: *an arranging of troops, battle array, arrangement, order, arranging,* taxis.

τάσσω (ταγ): *arrange, put in order, assign to a post.*

τάφος: *a grave, tomb.*

τείνω (τεν, τα): *stretch.*

τέκτων: *carpenter, builder, workman, craftsman.*

τέλος: *end, completion, purpose.*

τέμνω (τεμ): *cut.*

τέχνη: *art, skill, craft, trade.*

τῆλε: *far, afar.*

τίθημι (θε): *put, place.*

Τιτάν: *a* Titan.

Τιτανικός: *like a* Titan, Titanic.

τομή (τέμνω): *a cutting, a surgical operation; what is cut off, a stump, a section.*

τόμος: *a cut, slice, section; part of a book, volume,* tome.

τονικός (τόνος): *relating to tension, or tone,* tonic.

τόνος (τείνω): *a stretching, tension, tone,* tune.

τοξικός: *of or for the bow;* τοξικὸν φάρμακον: *poison for smearing arrows;* toxic, toxin.

τόξον: *a bow.*

τοπικός: *relating to a place, local,* topical.

τόπος: *place, position, part, passage in a book,* topic.

τραγικός: *of a goat, or of goats;* tragic. See τραγῳδία.

τράγος: *a goat.*

τραγῳδία (from τράγος and ἀείδω, *sing,* ἀοιδός, *singer*): *goat-song,* tragedy. The Greek tragedy grew out of the old dithyrambic songs which were sung by a chorus of satyrs, or goat-like creatures, and so could be called goat-song. The name tragedy was a survival from the early times and was retained after it was no longer appropriate in its etymological sense. The Greek tragedy of the classical period was a very serious composition and did not have a chorus of goats or satyrs, except in an afterpiece, or farce, which closed the day's performances.

τραχύς, fem. τραχεῖα: *rough.*
ἡ τραχεῖα <ἀρτηρία>: *the windpipe,* **trachea.**

τρέπω: *turn.*

τρέφω: *nourish, nurture.*

τρι-: prefix meaning *three,* being the stem of τρεῖς, *three.*

τρι-γωνο-μετρία: triangle-measurement, **trigonometry.**

τρί-γωνος: *having three angles, triangular;* in the neuter, *a triangle.*

τρί-πους, gen. τρί-ποδ-ος: *having three feet, three-legged; a three-legged stool, or table, a* **tripod.**

τροπαῖον (τροπή): a monument or sign which marked the spot where the enemy was routed, *a* **trophy.**

τροπή (τρέπω): *a turning; turning back of the sun, solstice, tropic; a turning, or routing of the enemy, rout, defeat.*

τρόπος: *a turn, way, manner; a turn of speech, figure of speech,* **trope.**

τύπος (τύπτω): *a blow, impression of a blow, imprint, mark, character, form, original form,* **type.**

τύπτω (τυπ): *strike, beat.*

τύραννος: *king,* **tyrant.**

τυρός: *cheese.*

Υ

Ὑάκινθος: **Hyacinthus,** a legendary youth beloved by the god Apollo and accidentally slain

by him. The **hyacinth,** a flower said to have sprung from the blood of Hyacinthus.

ὑγίεια: *health.*

ὑγιει-νός: *healthful, healthy,* **hygienic;** ὑγιεινή <τέχνη>: *the art or science of health,* **hygiene.**

ὑδατίς, gen. ὑδατίδ-ος (ὕδωρ): *a drop of water;* in med. *a watery vesicle, a* **hydatid.**

ὕδρα: *a water-serpent,* **hydra.**

ὑδραυλικός (ὕδραυλις): *of water-pipes;* ὑδραυλικὸν ὄργανον: a musical instrument with pipes operated by the movement of water, *a water-organ, hydraulic organ.* Hence English **hydraulic.**

ὕδρ-αυλις (ὕδωρ+αὐλός, *a pipe*): a musical instrument consisting of pipes made to sound by means of moving water, *a water-organ,* same as ὑδραυλικὸν ὄργανον. See section 134.

ὑδρο-στατικός (ἵστημι): having to do with standing water, **hydrostatic.**

ὑδρο-φοβία: *horror of water,* **hydrophobia.**

ὑδρο-φόβος (φοβέομαι): *having a horror of water.*

ὑδρο-φόρος (φέρω): *a water-carrier;* **hydrophore.**

ὕδωρ, gen. ὕδατ-ος: *water.* In compounds the stem usually takes the form ὑδρ- before vowels and ὑδρο- before consonants.

ὑμήν, gen. ὑμέν-ος: *a thin skin, membrane;* the hymen. Ὑμήν, Hymen, the god of marriage. Hence ὑμέναιος, *wedding-song, hymenaeus.* Eng. deriv. hymeneal.

ὕμνος: *a song of praise to gods and heroes, a* hymn.

ὑμν-ῳδία (ἀείδω): *hymn-singing,* hymnody.

ὑπέρ: *over, above, beyond, beyond due measure.*

ὑπερβάλλω: *throw beyond, exceed; throw beyond the mark, go to excess.*

ὑπερβολή: *excess, exaggeration,* hyperbole, hyperbola.

*ὑπερ-τροφία (τρέφω): *over-nourishment,* hypertrophy.

ὕπνος: *sleep.*

ὑπνόω: *put to sleep.*

*ὕπνωσις: *a state of sleep,* hypnosis.

ὑπνωτικός: *causing sleep,* hypnotic.

ὑπό: *under.*

ὑπό-θεσις (τίθημι): *a placing under, what is placed under, a foundation, supposition,* hypothesis.

ὑπο-θετικός: *of the nature of a hypothesis,* hypothetical.

ὑποκριτής: *an actor, pretender,* hypocrite.

ὑπο-τείνουσα (τείνω): *stretching under, subtending,* hypotenuse. This form is the feminine of the present participle of ὑποτείνω and agrees with the noun γραμμή, *a line.* ἡ ὑποτείνουσα γραμμή means literally *"the line stretching under."*

ὑπο-τείνω: *stretch under, subtend.*

*ὑπο-τροφία (τρέφω): *under-nourishment,* hypotrophy.

ὑπο-χόνδριος: *under the cartilage of the breastbone;* neut. ὑποχόνδριον, *the part of the body immediately under or below the cartilage of the breastbone.*

ὑφέν (ὑπο+ἑν, one): *under one, together; a sign for joining two words into one, a* hyphen.

Φ

φαγ (root of second aorist φαγεῖν, *to eat*): *eat, devour.*

φαινόμενον (φαίνομαι): *what is shown or appears, anything manifest to the senses,* phenomenon.

φαίνω (φαν), mid. and pass. φαίνομαι: *show, manifest; be shown, show itself, appear.*

φάλαγξ, gen. φάλαγγ-ος: *line of battle,* phalanx; *also a round piece of wood, a roller, the bone between two joints of the fingers and toes,* plural phalanges.

*φανερό-γαμος: *having visible marriage,* phanerogamous; *a* phanerogam.

φανερός (φαίνω): *shown, visible, manifest.*

φαντάζω (lengthened form from φαίνω): *make visible, make to appear;* mid. and pass. φαντάζομαι: *become visible, appear, take on an appearance, appear like, assume the appearance of.* φαντάζω and its derivatives often have in them the suggestion of an unreal, or deceptive, appearance unlike φαίνω which is used of real, or actual, manifestations.

φαντασία (φαντάζω): *appearance, imagination,* **fantasy, fancy.**

φάντασμα: *that which has appeared,* a **phantasm,** a **phantom.**

*φαντασμαγορία: *an assemblage of phantasms,* a **phantasmagory.**

φαρμακεία: *the use of drugs,* **pharmacy.**

φαρμακευ-τικός: *relating to drugs or pharmacy,* **pharmaceutic.**

φαρμακεύω: *drug, administer drugs, deal in drugs.*

φάρμακον: *a drug, medicine, philter, poison.*

φαρμακο-ποιία (ποιέω): *drug-making,* **pharmacopeia.**

φάρυγξ: *the throat, the* **pharynx.**

φάσις (for φάν-σις from φαίνω, stem φαν): *appearance,* **phase.**

φέρω: *bear, carry, bring.*

φημί (φα): *say, affirm.*

φθέγγομαι: *utter a sound, speak loud and clear.*

φθόγγος: *a sound, voice.*

φιλ-ανθρωπια: *love of human beings, humanity, benevolence,* **philanthropy.**

φιλ-άνθρωπος: *loving mankind, benevolent, humane,* **philanthropic.**

φιλέω: *love, be fond of, be a friend to.*

φίλ-ιππος (ἵππος): *loving horses, fond of horses;* **Philip.**

φιλό-δημος: *loving the people.*

φιλό-λογος: *loving speech or words, fond of literature; a student of language and literature,* a **philologue, philologist.**

φιλο-μαθής (μάθος, μανθάνω): *fond of learning; a person who is fond of learning,* a **philomath.**

φίλος: *friend, lover.*

φιλο-σοφία: *love of wisdom,* **philosophy.**

φιλό-σοφος: *a lover of wisdom,* **philosopher.**

φλέγω: *burn, flame, blaze.*

φλέψ, gen. φλεβ-ός: *a vein.*

φλόξ, gen. φλογ-ός (φλέγω): *a flame, blaze,* **phlox.**

φοβέομαι: *be afraid, fear.*

φόβος: *fear, dread, terror.*

φοῖβος, fem. φοίβη: *pure, bright, radiant;* used as an epithet of Apollo and his twin sister Artemis, so that Apollo was often called Φοῖβος, **Phoebus,** and Artemis Φοίβη, **Phoebe.**

φράγμα (φράσσω): *fence, screen, defence.*

φράζω (φραδ): *show, tell, declare.*

φράσις: *utterance, expression,* phrase, phraseology.

φράσσω (φραγ): *build a fence, fence in,* fortify.

φύλαξις: *a watching, guarding,* phylaxis.

φυλάσσω (φυλακ): *guard, protect.*

φύλλον: *a leaf.*

φῦλον: *a race, a tribe.*

φυσικός: *relating to nature, natural,* physical.

φυσιολογία: *study of nature, natural philosophy,* physiology.

φυσιολόγος (φύσις+λέγω): *one who discourses about nature, a natural philosopher, a* physiologist.

φύσις (φύω): *growing, what grows, nature.*

φυτόν: *that which has grown, a plant, a tree.*

φύω: *grow.*

φωνή: *sound, voice.*

φῶς, *gen.* φωτ-ός: *light.*

φωσ-φόρος (φέρω): *light-bearing; a light-bearer.* Eng. deriv. phosphorous.

X

χαίτη: *hair,* especially *long flowing hair.*

χάος: chaos.

χαρακτήρ (χαράσσω): *a mark, impress, stamp,* character.

χαράσσω (χαρακ): *scratch, furrow, engrave.*

χάσμα: *a yawning, a* chasm.

χείρ: *hand.*

*χειρο-μαντεία (μάντις): *fortune-telling from the hand, palmistry,* chiromancy.

χειρουργία (ἐργ, *work*): *a working with the hand, handicraft;* in medicine, *operating with the hand,* surgery, chirurgery.

χειρουργικός: *relating to surgery,* surgical, chirurgical.

χειρουργός:. *a handworker, a* surgeon, chirurgeon.

χίμαιρα: *a she-goat; a fabulous monster part lion, part goat, and part serpent;* hence English chimera, and chimerical.

χλωρός: *light green, green.*

χοάνη (χέω): *a funnel.*

χόνδρος: *groat, grit, lump; gristle,* cartilage.

χορδή: *a gut, a string made of gut for a lyre or harp, a* chord, *a cord.*

χορός: *a dancing place, a dance, a band of dancers and singers, a* chorus, choir.

χριστός (χρίω): *anointed;* ὁ Χριστός, *the anointed one,* Christ.

χρίω: *anoint.*

χρονικός: *relating to time; of long duration,* chronic.

χρόνος: *time.*

χρυσός: *gold.*

χρῶμα: *color,* chrome.

Ψ

ψάλλω: *twang a bow string, play a lyre, or harp.*

ψάλμα: *a tune played on the harp, or lyre.*

ψαλμός: *a song sung to the music of the harp, a* psalm.

ψεῦδος: *a falsehood, lie.*

ψυχή: *breath, life, soul, spirit, mind.*

Ω

ᾠδή (contracted form of ἀοιδή from ἀείδω, *sing*): *song,* ode.

ᾠδεῖον: *place of song, music hall,* odeum.

ὠθέω (ὠθ): *push, thrust, shove.*

ᾠόν: *egg.*

ὥρα: *season,* hour.

ὠσμός (ὠθέω): *a pushing, thrusting, shoving.*

*ὤσμωσις: *a pushing,* osmosis.

VI. INDEX AND KEY TO DERIVATION

144. The Greek words are intended to suggest the derivation of the English words which they follow. These Greek words and the words related to them should be looked up in the vocabulary by anyone who wishes to trace the derivation of the English words. The numbers refer to sections in this book.

acme, ἀκμή
acoustic, ἀκουστικός
acrobat, ἀκροβατής
acrobatic
aeronaut 34, 79, ἀήρ, ναύτης
aesthetic 43, 84, αἰσθητικός
agnostic 41, ἀγνωστικός
agonize, ἀγωνιάω
agony, ἀγωνία
agronomy 121
alms, ἐλεημοσύνη
alphabet 1
amethyst, ἀμέθυστος
amoeba, ἀμοιβή
amorphous 107
amphioxus, ἀμφί, ὀξύς
amphitheater 51, 100, III (b)
anabolic 117, ἀναβολικός
anabolism 117, ἀναβολισμός
anaemia (anemia), ἀν-, αἷμα
anaesthesia 77, ἀναισθησία
anaesthetic 53, 84
analgesia, ἀναλγησία
analogous 129, ἀνάλογος
analysis 77. ἀνάλυσις
analytic, analytical 84
anarchy 116
anathema 51, ἀνα, τίθημι

anatomy 75, ἀνατομή
anecdote 83
anemometer ἄνεμος, μέτρον
anemone, ἀνεμώνη
angel 10
angiosperm, ἀγγεῖον, σπέρμα
anodyne 53
anomalous, ἀνώμαλος
anomaly, ἀνωμαλία
anonymous, ἀν-, ὄνυμα; see ὄνομα
antagonism 96 (f)
antagonist 96 (f), ἀνταγωνιστής
antagonistic 96 (f)
antagonize 96 (f), ἀνταγωνίζομαι
antarctic, ἀντί, ἄρκτος
anthem, ἀντίφωνος
anther 38
anthophorous, ἄνθος, φέρω
anthropoid 94
anthropology, ἄνθρωπος, λέγω
anthropomorphism, ἄνθρωπος, μορφή
antidote 42, 51, 83
antinomy 121
antistrophe, ἀντί, στροφή
antithesis 111
antithetic 111

antitoxin, ἀντί, τοξικός
apathetic 53, 118
apathy 118, ἀπάθεια
apheresis 101
apology 51, ἀπολογία
apostasy 51, 112
apostate 112, ἀποστάτης
apostle, ἀπόστολος
apostrophe, ἀποστροφή
apothecary 111
apothegm, ἀπόφθεγμα
aptera, ἀ-, πτέρον
arachnida, ἀράχνη
archaeologist 116
archaeology 116
archaic 116
archangel 116
archetype 116
archiblast 116
architect 116
architectonic 116
archives 116
arctic, ἄρκτος
argon 135
argonaut 79
aristocracy 47, 131
aristocrat 131
aristocratic 131
arithmetic 32, 92, 96 (b)
artery, ἀρτηρία
arthritis 93, 110
arthropoda, ἄρθρον, πούς
arthrosis 73, 110
article 48
asbestos, ἄσβεστος
ascetic, ἀσκητικός
aseptic 53
aspirates 64 (1)
aster, ἀστήρ
asteroid 94
asthenia, ἀσθένεια
asthma, ἄσθμα

astrologer 85, 86, 100, III (a), 102, 124
astrological 124
astrologize 103
astrology 86, 102, 103, 124
astronomer 121, 103 note
astronomize 103
astronomy 103, 121
asylum, ἄσυλος
atheism, ἀ-, θεός
athlete 76
atmosphere, ἀτμός, σφαῖρα
atom, ἄτομος
atrophy, ἀτροφία
authentic, αὐθεντικός
autobiography, αὐτός, βίος, γράφω
autocracy 131
autocratic, αὐτός, κράτος
autograph 47
automatic, αὐτοματικός
automaton, αὐτόματος
autopsy 45, αὐτοψία
axiom, ἀξίωμα
azygos, ἄζυγος

barbarian 96 (f)
barbarism 77, 96 (f)
barbarize 77, 96 (f)
baritone (barytone), βαρύτονος
barometer, βάρος, μέτρον
base, basis 36
Bible, βιβλίον
bibliotheca 111, βιβλιοθήκη
biographer 85, 86
biography 86
biologize 127
biology, βίος, λέγω
bionomics, βίος, νόμος
bishop 139, ἐπίσκοπος
botany, βοτάνη
brachiopod, βραχίων, πούς

bronchia 10
bronchitis 93
bucolic, βουκολικός
butter, βούτυρον

calisthenics 53, καλλι-, σθένος
calligraphy, καλλι-, γράφω
calyx, κάλυξ
canon 34
carcinoma, καρκίνος
cardiac 90
carpophore, καρπός, φέρω
catabolic 117
catabolism 117
catalepsy, κατάληψις
catalog 51, κατάλογος
cataract 51, καταράσσω
catarrh 71, κατάρροος
catastrophe 51, καταστροφή
category, κατηγορία
cathedral, καθέρδα
Catholic, καθολικός
caustic, καυστικός
cauterize, καυτηριάζω
cemetery, κοιμη-τήριον
cenotaph, κενός, τάφος
center, κέντρον
chaetognatha, χαίτη, γνάθος
chaos, χάος
chaotic
character, χαρακτήρ
characterize
chasm, χάσμα
chirography 34, χείρ
chiromancy 108, χειρομαντεία
chirurgery 135
chirurgical 135
chlorophyll, χλωρός, φύλλον
choanocyte, χοάνη, κύτος
choir, χορός
chondrectomy, χόνδρος, ἐκ, τέμνω
chondrotome, χόνδρος, τέμνω

chord, χορδή
chorus 22
Christ, χρίω, χριστός
chronic, χρονικός
chronology, χρόνος, λέγω
chronometer, χρόνος, μέτρον
chrysanthemum, χρυσός, ἄνθεμον
cladophyl, κλάδος, φύλλον
cleptocratic 131
cleptomania, κλέπτης, μανία
climax 34
clinic, κλινικός
coelenterata, κοῖλος, ἔντερον
coelomata, κοίλωμα
coleoptera, κολεός, πτέρον
colon, κῶλον
comedy, κωμῳδία
comet, κομήτης
comic, κωμικός
comma, κόμμα
compound words 62, 98 ff.
cord, χορδή
Corinth 89
Corinthian 89
corruptions 139
cosmetic 96 (b)
cosmogony, κόσμος, γίγνομαι
cosmopolitan 32
cosmos, κόσμος
cotyledon, κοτυληδών
crasis, κράσις
crater 76
crisis 41, 77
critic 30
critical 41
crocus, κρόκος
crypt 83
cryptogam 83
cryptogram 41, 83
crystal, κρύσταλλος
ctenophore, κτείς, φέρω
cube, κύβος

cyclamen, κυκλάμινος
cycle, κύκλος
cylinder, κύλινδρος
cynosure, κυνός-ουρα
Cyrus 22
cyst, cystis, κύστις
cystectomy, κύστις, ἐκτέμνω
cyte, κύτος
cytoblast, κύτος, βλαστός
cytogenesis, κύτος, γένεσις
cytoplasm, κύτος, πλάσμα

dacryrrhea, δακρύρροια
deacon, διάκονος
deleterious, δηλέομαι
demagogic 133
demagogue 133
demagogy 133
democracy 131
democrat 131
democratic 38, 131
demon 34
denominative 60
dermatology 34
despot, δεσπότης
despotic
despotism
deuteroplasm, δεύτερος, πλάσμα
devil 139, διάβολος
diadem, διάδημα
diagonal, διάγωνος
diagram, διά, γράφω
dialect 129, διαλέγομαι
dialectic 129
dialogue 129
diameter 51
diaphanous 119
diaphragm 51
diarrhea, διάρροια
diarthrosis 110
diastase 112
diastasis 112

diastatic 112
diastem 112
diathesis 111
diathetic 111
didactic, διδάσκω
dieresis 101
diet 30, δίαιτα
dilemma 53, δίλημμα
diocese, διοίκεσις
diosmosis, διά, ὠσμός
diphtheria, διφθέρα
diphthong 12, 53
diploma, δίπλωμα
diplomat
diplomatic
diptera, δι-, πτέρον
dogma 34, 132
dogmatic 132
dogmatism 132
dogmatist 132
dogmatize 132
dose 42
double consonants 64 (4)
doxology 132
drachm, δραχμή
drama 34, 41, 78
drastic, δραστικός
dryad, δρύς
dynamic 36, 44
dynamite, δύναμις
dynamo (dynamo-electric machine), δύναμις
dynasty 44, δυναστεία
dysentery 53, δυς-, ἔντερον
dyspepsia 41, 53

eccentric 51, ἐκκεντρικός
echo, ἠχώ
eclectic 130
eclogue 130
ecology, οἶκος, λέγω
economic 121

economics 121
economist 121
economize 121
economy 20, 104, 121
ecstasy 112
ecstatic 112
-ectomy, ἐκτομή, ἐκτέμνω
egoism 49
egoistic 49
egotism 49
egotistic 49
elastic, ἐλαστικός
electric 136, ἤλεκτρον
electrolysis 41
electro-magnet, ἤλεκτρον, Μαγνῆτις
elegiac, ἐλεγειακός
elegy, ἐλεγεῖον
elephant, ἔλεφας
emblem 117
embryo, ἔμβρυον
emphasis 119
emphatic 119
emporium, ἐμπόριον
encaustic 51, ἐν, καυστικός
encephalus 19, ἐγκέφαλος
enchiridion 19, ἐγχειρίδιον
encomium 10
endemic, ἐν, δῆμος
endocarp, ἔνδον, καρπός
endogen 52
endosmosis, ἔνδον, ὦσμωσις
energetic 135
energy 51, 135
enhydrous 51, ἐν, ὕδωρ
enigma, αἴνιγμα
enthusiasm, ἐνθουσιασμός
enthusiast, ἐνθουσιαστής
enthusiastic, ἐνθουσιαστικός
entomology, ἔντομον, λέγω
entomostraca, ἔντομον, ὄστρακον
ephemeral, ἐπί, ἡμέρα

epiblast, ἐπί, βλαστός
epic, ἐπικός
epidemic, ἐπί, δῆμος
epidermis 51, ἐπί, δέρμα
epigram 51, 78, ἐπίγραμμα
epigrammatic, ἐπιγραμματ-ικός
epigraphy, ἐπιγραφή
epileptic 65
epilepsy 101
epilogue 129, ἐπίλογος
epiphyte 83
Episcopalian, ἐπίσκοπος
episode, ἐπεισόδιον
epistle, ἐπιστολή
epitaph 51, ἐπί, τάφος
epithem 111
epithesis 111
epithet 83, 111
epitome, ἐπιτομή
epizoön, ἐπί, ζῷον
epoch, ἐποχή
ergograph 135, end
erythrocyte, ἐρυθρός, κύτος
esophagus, οἴσω, φαγ
esoteric 52
ether, αἰθήρ
ethics 92, ἠθικός
ethnic, ἐθνικός
ethnology, ἔθνος, λέγω
Eugene 94
eugenic 43, 94
eulogist 129
eulogistic 129
eulogize 129
eulogy 129
-eum 81
euphony 52, 63
evangelical, εὐαγγέλιον
evangelist
evangelize, εὐαγγελίζομαι
exocarp, ἔξω, καρπός
exodus 51, ἔξοδος

exogen 52, ἔξω, γίγνομαι
exoteric 52
exosmosis, ἐξ, ὦσμωσις

fancy 119
fantastic 119
fantasy 119

galaxy, γαλαξίας
gastrectomy, γαστήρ, ἐκτομή
gastric, γαστρικός
gastrology, γαστήρ, λέγω
genealogy 30, γενεαλογία
genesis 36
genetic 43
geocentric, γέα, κέντρον
geode 94
geodesy 114
geodetic 114
geographer 100, III (a), 102, 114
geography 41, 102, 114
geologist 114
geology 114
geometer 114
geometric 114
geometry 114
George 114
Georgia 114
georgic 114
geotropism, γέα, τρέπω
geranium, γεράνιον
gigantic 34
glossary, γλῶσσα
grammar, γραμματική
grammatical, γραμματικός
graphic, γραφικός
gymnasium 96 (e)
gymnast 96 (e)
gymnastic 96 (e)
gymnosperm, γυμνός, σπέρμα

harmony, ἁρμονία
hectic 65
heliocentric, ἥλιος, κέντρον
heliograph 32
heliotrope 72
Hellene 96 (f)
Hellenic 96 (f)
Hellenism 96 (f)
Hellenist 96 (f)
Hellenistic 96 (f)
Hellenize 96 (f)
hematocytolysis, αἷμα, κύτος, λύσις
hematophyte, αἷμα, φυτόν
hematorrhea, αἷμα, ῥέω
hemisphere 53
hemorrhage, αἱμορραγία
hepatic 34
hepatica, ἡπατικός
heresy 101
heretic, αἱρετικός
hermit (eremite), ἐρημίτης
hero, ἥρως
heroic, ἡρωικός
heterodox 132
heterodoxy 132
hierarch 116
hierarchy 116
hierophant 44
hippodrome 32
hippopotamus, ἵππος, ποταμός
history 30, ἱστορία
hodometer, ὁδός, μέτρον
holocaust, ὅλος, καίω
homogeneous 38, 47, 94, 100, III (c)
homonym, ὁμός, ὄνυμα, ὄνομα
horizon, ὁρίζων
horoscope, ὥρα, σκοπός
hyacinth, ὑάκινθος
hydatid, ὑδατίς
hydr-, ὕδωρ

hydra 134
hydrangea, ὕδωρ, ἀγγεῖον
hydrant 134
hydrate 134
hydraulic 134 *and note*
hydro- 134
hydrocyst, ὕδωρ, κύστις
hydrogen, ὕδωρ, γίγνομαι
hydromedusa, ὕδωρ, Μέδουσα
hydrometer, ὕδωρ, μέτρον
hydrophobia 134
hydrophore 104
hydrostatic 112, 134
hydrotomy, ὕδωρ, τέμνω
hygiene 30, ὑγ'εινός
hymenoptera, ὑμήν, πτέρον
hymn, ὕμνος
hymnody, ὑμνῳδία
hyperbole 51, 117
hypercritical 51
hypertrophy, ὑπέρ, τρέφω
hyphen, ὑφέν
hypnosis, ὑπνόω
hypoblast, ὑπό, βλαστός
hypochondriac, ὑποχόνδριος
hypodermic 51, ὑπό, δέρμα
hypotenuse, ὑποτείνουσα
hypothesis 51, 111
hypothetical 111
hypotrophy, ὑπο, τρέφω

-ic 90
-ical 91
ichthyology 36
ichthyohagous 45
iconoclast, εἰκών, κλάω
-ics 92
idea 30
idiom, ἰδίωμα
idiomatic
idiosyncrasy, ἰδιοσυγκρασία
idol, εἴδωλον

idolatry, εἰδωλο-λατρεία
idyl, εἰδύλλιον
idyllic, εἰδυλλικός
Irene, εἰρήνη
irenic, εἰρηνικός
iris, ἶρις
-ism 97
isotherm, ἴσος, θερμός
-ist 97
-istic 97
-itis 93
-ize 95, 97

kaleidoscope 38

labials 64 (1)
laconic, Λακωνικός
larynx 34
lemma, λῆμμα
lethargy, ληθαργία
leucocyte, λευκός, κύτος
lexicon 129
liquids 64 (1), (2)
lithograph 32
liturgy, λειτουργία
logic 92, 129
logical 129
logographer 129
logography 129
lyre, λύρα
lyric, λυρικός

magic, μαγικός
malacostraca, μαλακός, ὄστρακον
mania 108
maniac 108
martyr, μάρτυς
mausoleum 81
mechanic 30
megaphone 47
melancholy 47
melodrama, μέλος, δρᾶμα

melody, μελῳδία
mesentery, μεσεντέριον
mesoblast, μέσος, βλαστός
mesocarp, μέσος, καρπός
Mesopotamia, μέσος, ποταμός
metabolic 117
metabolism 117
metacarpus 51, καρπός
metallurgy 135
metamorphic 107
metamorphose 51, 107
metamorphosis 107
metamorphous 107
metaphor, μεταφορά
metaphysics 140, μετά, φυσικά
metathesis 111
meteor, μετέωρος
meter, μέτρον
method 32, μετά, ὁδός
Methodist, method
metonymy, μετά, ὄνομα
metrical, μέτρον
metronome, μέτρον, νέμω
metropolis 100, III (b)
miasma, μίασμα
miasmatic, μιασματικός
microbe, μικρός, βίος
microscope 47
microtome 41, 47
mime 109
mimeograph, μιμέομαι, γράφω
mimesis 109
mimetic 43, 109
mimic 109
misanthrope 123
misanthropic 123
misanthropy, μισέω, ἄνθρωπος
misogynism 123
misogynist 123
misogyny 123
monarch. μόνος, ἄρχω, μόναρ-
χος

monarchy, μοναρχία
monk, μοναχός
monogram 78
monolith 32
monopoly, μονοπωλία
monosyllable, μόνος, συλλαβή
monotone 46
monotonous 100, III (c)
Morpheus 107
morphine 107
morphosis 107
museum 22, 81
music 74, 92
mutes 64 (1)
mycetozoön, μύκης, ζῷον
myelitis, μύελος
myelocyst, μύελος, κύστις
myelocyte, μύελος, κύτος
mystery, μυστήριον
mystic, μυστικός
myth 22, 124
mythic 106
mythological 106, 124
mythologist 85, 86
mythology 86, 106, 124

naiad, Ναϊάς
narcissus, νάρκισσος
narcosis 96 (c)
narcotic 96 (c)
nausea, ναυσία
nautical 79
necromancy 108
necropolis, νεκρός, πόλις
necrosis 96 (c)
nectar, νέκταρ
nemesis 121
neolithic 47
neophyte 47, 83
nephritis 74, 93
neuralgia, νεῦρον, ἄλγος
neurasthenia, νεῦρον, ἀσθένεια

neuraxon, νεῦρον, ἄξων
neurocyte, νεῦρον, κύτος
neurology, νεῦρον, λέγω
neuroma, νεῦρον
neuron 136
neurosis, νεῦρον
neurotic, νεῦρον
nomad 121
nomadic 121
nome 121
nosology 32
notochord, νῶτον, χορδή
nymph, νύμφη

ochlocracy 131
ode, ᾠδή
odeum 81
oid 94
oligarch, ὀλίγος, ἄρχω
-ology 86, 87, 122, 125
Olympian 89
Olympus 89
oöspore, ᾠόν, σπόρος
optical, ὀπτικός
optician, ὀπτικός
optics 45
orchestra, ὀρχήττρα
organ 32, 135 and note
organic 135
organism 135
organize 135
ornithology 34
orphan, ὀρφανός
orthodox 132
orthodoxy 132
orthography, ὀρθός, γράφω
orthoptera, ὀρθός, πτέρον
-osis 96 (c)
osmosis. ὥσμωσις
ostracize, ὀστρακίζω
otology 34, οὖς, λέγω
oxygen, ὀξύς, γίγνομαι

pachyderm 34
pachydermous 100, III (c)
paedeutic 96 (d)
palatals 64 (1)
panacea, πανάκεια
panorama 41
pantheism 47
pantograph 47
pantomime 109
paradigm 67
paradise, παράδεισος
paradox 132
paradoxical 132
paragraph 51
parallel, παράλληλος
paralysis, παρά, λύω
paraphrase, παράφρασις
parasite 51, παράσιτος
parenthesis 111
parenthetical 111
pathetic 118
pathological 118
pathology 38, 118
pathos 118
patriarch 116
patriarchy, πατριαρχία
patriot 79
pedagogical 133
pedagogue 34, 133
pedagogy 133
pediatric 34
pediatry, παῖς, ἰατρεία
pentagon, πεντάγωνος
peony, παιώνιος
pepsin 41
perianth, περί, ἄνθος
pericardium, περί, καρδία
pericarp 51, περί, καρπός
perimeter 51
period, περίοδος
periodic, περιοδ-ικός
periphrasis, περίφρασις

perisarc, περί, σάρξ
peristyle, περίστυλον
peritoneum, περιτόναιον
petal, πέταλον
phagocyte, φαγ, κύτος
phalanx, φάλαγξ
phanerogam 119
phantasm 119
phantasmagory 119
phantom 119
pharmaceutic 96 (d)
pharmacopeia, φαρμακοποιία
pharmacy 32
pharynx, φάρυγξ
phase 119
phenomenon 20, 44, 119
Philadelphia 32
philanthropic 122
philanthropist 122
philanthropy 122
philharmonic 122
Philip 122, φίλιππος
philodemic 122
philologist 122
philology 122
philomath 122
philosopher 122
philosophy 80, 122
phlebotomy 34, φλέψ, τέμνω
phlox, φλόξ
phonetic, φωνή, φωνέω
phonograph, φωνή, γράφω
phosphorous 85
photograph 34
photographer 85, 86
photography 86
photosphere, φῶς, σφαῖρα
phyllophorous, φύλλον, φέρω
phyllopoda, φύλλον, ποῖς
phylum, φῦλον
physical 36, 90
physician, φυσικός

physics 36, 92, 136
physiography, φύσις, γράφω
physiological 124
physiologize 124
physiology 124, 136
-phyte 83
pirate 96 (a)
piratical 96 (a)
plague, πληγή
planet, πλάνης
plasm 67
plaster, ἔμπλαστρον
plastic 66
plethora, πληθώρη
pleura, πλευρά
plutocracy 131
pneumatic, πνευματικός
pneumonia, πνεύμων
poem 78
poet 30, 41, 73, 76
polemic, πολεμικός
poliomyelitis, πολιός, μύελος
political 79, 90
politics 36, 79, 92
polyanthous 38
polygamous 80, 85, 86
polygamy 80, 86
polyglot, πολύς, γλῶττα = γλῶσσα
polygon, πολύγωνος
polymorphous 107
polypus 34
polytechnic, πολύς, τέχνη
polytheism 47
pomp 75
pore, πόρος
practical 65, 84, 120
practice 120
pragmatic 40, 41, 120
praxis 120
prefix 58
Presbyterian, πρεσβύτερος
priest, 139, πρεσβύτερος

prism, πρίσμα
problem 117
problematic 117
prognathous 32
prologue 51, 129
propaedeutic 96 (*d*)
prophet 51, πρό, φημί
prophylaxis, πρό, φυλάσσω
protagonist, πρωταγωνιστής
protoplasm, πρῶτος, πλάσμα
protozoön, πρῶτος, ζῷον
psalm, ψαλμός
pseudonym 38
pseudopodia, ψεῦδος, πούς
psychiatry, ψυχή, ἰατρεία
psychotherapy, ψυχή, θεραπεία
ptomaine, πτῶμα
pyosis 96 (*c*)
pyramid, πυραμίς
pyre, πυρή
pyrography, πῦρ, γράφω
pyrosis 96 (*c*)
pyrotechnic 34

rhetor 19, 76
rhetoric 92
rhetorical 90
rhinoceros, ῥινοκέρως
rhinology 34
rhododendron, ῥόδον, δένδρον
rhythm, ῥυθμός
rhythmical, ῥυθμικός
root 55

sarcasm, σαρκασμός
sarcastic, σαρκαστικός
sarcoma, σάρξ
sarcophagus 45, σάρξ, φαγ
satyr, σάτυρος
scandal, σκάνδαλον
scene, σκηνή
scenic, σκηνικός

scepter 32
scheme, σχῆμα
schism 41, 113
schismatic 113
schist 113
schistocyte 113
schistoglossia 113
scholar, σχολή, Latin scholaris, *scholaris*
scholastic 66
scholium, σχόλιον from σχολή
school 30, σχολή
sclerosis 96 (*c*)
sclerotic 96 (*c*)
scope, σκοπός
semaphore 41
sepsis 77
septic 84
sibilant 64 (3)
simple word 61
skeleton 83
skeptic 43
sonants 64 (1)
sophism 67, 96 (*f*)
sophist 96 (*f*)
sophistic 96 (*f*)
spasm, σπασμός
spasmodic 94
sphere, σφαῖρα
spheroid 94
sphincter, σφιγκτήρ
sphinx, σφίγξ
sphygmic, σφυγμός
sphygmograph 77
spleen, σπλήν
sporadic, σπορά, σποράδην, σπο-
ραδικός
spore, σπόρος
static 42, 112
stem 56
stereoscope, στερεός, σκοπός
stereopticon, στερεός, ὀπτικός

stereotype, στερεός, τύπος
sternum 22
stigma, στίγμα
stomach, στόμαχος
story, shortened form of history,
  ἱστορία
stratagem 133
strategic 133
strategy 100, III (a), 102, 133
strophe, στροφή
suffix 57
surds 64 (1)
surgeon 135, 139
surgery 135
surgical 135
syllable 70, 101
sylloge 130
symbol 117
symmetry, συμμετρία, συν+μέτ-
  ρον
sympathetic 118
sympathize 118
sympathy 68, 118
symphony 68
symphysis 68
symptom, σύμπτωμα
symptomatic, συμπτωματ-ικός
synagogue, συναγωγή
synarthrosis 110
synchondrosis, σύν, χόνδρος
syndesmosis, συνδέσμωσις
synod, σύνοδος
synonym, σύν, ὄνομα
syntactical 115
syntax 115
synthesis 42, 77, 111
synthetic 111
syringe, σῦριγξ
system 70, 73, 78, 112
systematic 112
systematize 112

tactical 115
tactics 115
taxonomy, τάξις, νόμος
technical, τεχνικός, τέχνη
telegram 78
telegraph 52
telephone, τῆλε, φωνέω
telescope 43, 100, III (b)
theater 32, θέατρον
theism 32, θεός
theme 111
theologian 124
theological 124
theology 124
theorem, θεώρημα
theoretical, θεωρητικός
theory, θεωρία
theosophy, θεός, σοφία
therapeutic, θεραπευτικός
therapy, θεραπεία
thermometer, θερμός, μέτρον
thesis 111
thoracic, θωρακ-ικός, θῶραξ
thorax, θῶραξ
-tic 84
titanic, τιτανικός
tome 75
tone 72, 75
tonic, τονικός
topic, τοπικός, τόπος
topography, τόπος, γράφω
toxic, τοξικός
toxin, τοξικός
trachea, τραχύς
tragedy, τραγῳδία
tragic, τραγικός
trichina 34, θρίξ
trichoblast 34, θρίξ, βλαστός
tricycle, τρι-, κύκλος
trigonometry, τριγωνομετρία
tripod, 34, 100, III (c)

trope 75
trophy, τροπαῖον
tropic 41, 72, 75
tune, τόνος
type 32, 41
typical, τυπικός, τύπος
tyrannical, τυρανν-ικός, τύραννος
tyranny, τυρανν-ίς, τύραννος
tyrant, τύραννος

verbal 59

xiphoid, ξιφοειδής
xiphosura, ξίφος, οὐρα

zone, ζωνή
zoölogist 85, 86, 102
zoölogize 127
zoölogy 86, 102
zoöphyte, ζῷον, φυτόν